LOOK AT YOUR
WORLD

LOOK AT YOUR WORLD

PAUL H. DUNN
MAURINE WARD

Bookcraft
Salt Lake City, Utah

Library of Congress Catalog Card Number 78-66824
ISBN O-88494-353-4

5 6 7 8 9 10   89 88 87 86 85 84 83

Lithographed in the United States of America
PUBLISHERS PRESS
Salt Lake City, Utah

Preface

I have long felt that true religion should be practical. Correct gospel principles would naturally solve problems and at the same time give encouragement and direction.

This volume attempts to look at the world and its many challenges and to suggest ways of meeting those challenges in a practical "down-to-earth" way. It is hoped that the reader will find new desire in solving old problems in applying some of the concepts taught here.

I am grateful to Maurine Ward for her insight and creativity in assisting in this work. She is a most unusual writer.

A special thanks to David Christensen for great ideas and sound principles.

Thanks also to Sharene Miner Hansen, my secretary, for her usual effectiveness in typing and proofreading.

I am particularly grateful to my wife, Jeanne, for her constant support and encouragement and for her editorial comments and suggestions.

I always appreciate the support of my daughters, Janet, Marsha, Kellie, and their families.

PAUL H. DUNN

Contents

LOOK AROUND YOU

LOOK WITHIN

LOOK TO THE LIGHT

Look to the Future

1

Focus Your Energies

There's a funny kind of insect called a processionary caterpillar that feeds upon pine needles. (That's a sharp diet.) In a group these insects move through the trees in a long procession, one leading, the others following—each with his eyes half-closed and his head snugly fitted against the rear extremity of his predecessor.

I once read a story about these strange little beasts.

"Jean-Henri Fabre, the great French naturalist, after patiently experimenting with a group of these caterpillars, finally enticed them to the rim of a large flowerpot where he succeeded in getting the first one connected up with the last one, thus forming a complete circle which started moving around in a procession which had neither beginning nor end.

"The Naturalist expected that after a while they would catch on to the joke—get tired of their useless march and start off in some new direction. But not so.

"Through sheer force of habit, the living, creeping circle kept moving around the rim of the flowerpot—around and around, keeping the same relentless pace for seven days and seven nights—and would doubtless have continued longer had it not been for sheer exhaustion and ultimate starvation.

"Incidentally, an ample supply of food was close at hand and plainly visible, but it was outside the range of the circle; so they continued along the beaten path.

"They were following instinct—habit, custom, tradition, precedent, past experience, 'standard practice,' or whatever you may choose to call it— but they were following it blindly.

"They mistook activity for accomplishment. They meant well—but they got no place." (As quoted in *Old Testament: Teacher Manual* [Provo, Utah: Department of Seminaries and Institutes of Religion, 1971], p. 19/13.)

Ever feel a little like these caterpillars, like you're going around in circles but getting nowhere? Too many of us, as Rufus Jones said, substitute speed for direction.

We greatly admire the man or woman who, as they say, is going places. But have you stopped lately and wondered just where *you* are headed? It's too easy to dissipate our energies in random activities that don't amount to much. Passive, we are often content to sit back, yawn, and spend the precious years of our lives on what seems easiest, or what seems most expedient, or just what's on TV.

If we live life without purpose, we live it without passion, and our days fall bland and tasteless on our souls.

Have you noticed the sunlight on a winter's day? That incredible fiery energy hardly penetrates the chill, and our toes freeze on the sunniest day. But take a magnifying glass, hold it over a piece of paper on the sidewalk and focus that massive energy, and you can char the paper black. Cold bones or a warm fire? The focus made all the difference.

Someone has said, "The longer I lived, the more deeply I am convinced that that which makes the difference between one man and another, between the weak and the powerful, the great and the insignificant, is energy, invincible determination—the purpose once formed, and then death or victory." Mark Twain felt much the same and expressed himself in this way, "If I were heathen, I would build a statue to energy and fall down and worship it."

A man was once listening to an outstanding concert pianist play a sonata on the piano. "I would give anything in the world to be able to play like that," he said.

"All right," the pianist responded. "Let's see if you really mean that. You say that you would give anything in the world to be able to play as I have. I have given several hours a day almost every day for the last fifteen years. I have given up picnics and parties and many other kinds of entertainment in order to stay at my task. I have sacrificed the study of many interesting subjects; I have given and worked and worked and given until at times it seemed that I could not work another hour or sacrifice another thing. To play the piano as well as I do, would you be willing to give that much?"

"You've got me there," he admitted. "I thought I would give anything to be a great piano player. I realize now that, while I would give up a few things, I do not want this particular ability enough to sacrifice much time or many pleasures for its attainment."

Again, a man can learn to lift four or five times what a normal man could press when he gives up other things and focuses his energies on muscle development.

Well, proficiency at the piano or weight lifting may not be a driving goal in your life, but I hope for your sake that excellence in something is. I hope that you ache and yearn and push toward an end that really matters to you.

Otherwise you're in danger of becoming the kind of person Goethe described when he said, "He's a dull man; if he were a book I wouldn't read him."

When you find yourself saying, "What's the use?" "Why bother?" or "Why should I?" you've guaranteed yourself a life of mediocrity and misery. You've stunted all your possibilities.

"Energy, invincible determination, and then death or victory." Such is the law of success in every sphere of life. Why should it not be so in the building of a righteous character? In Matthew we read, "Blessed are they which do hunger and thirst after righteousness: for they shall be filled." (Matthew 5:6.)

Hunger. Thirst. What vivid, dramatic words are these. Have you ever gone without water for a day, felt your tongue grow swollen and parched in your mouth until you felt you'd give up anything for one sweet drop of liquid?

How much more must those who lived in the semidesert land of Palestine, those people to whom the Bible was addressed, have felt that anguish for water.

Perhaps the most poetic Old Testament writer, the Psalmist, yearns: "As the hart panteth after the water brooks, so panteth my soul after thee, O God. My soul thirsteth for God, for the living God." (Psalm 42:1-2.)

Isaiah, searching for words to describe the happy future of Zion, tells his people: "For in the wilderness shall waters break out, and streams in the desert. And the parched ground shall become a pool, and the thirsty land springs of water." (Isaiah 35:6-7.)

John the Revelator even goes so far as to compare heaven to a place containing a crystal spring of water where one may drink as much as he pleases without charge. "I will give unto him that is athirst of the fountain of the water of life freely." (Revelation 21:6.)

Hungry, so hungry your stomach clamors in pain for food; thirsty, so thirsty your tongue sticks to your teeth. The Lord told the Nephites, "And blessed are all they who do hunger and thirst after righteousness, for they shall be filled with the Holy Ghost." (3 Nephi 12:6.)

The history of our times may record this people as a desire-driven mob living in the most affluent society man has produced. But I see us instead as a people whose desires are too easily filled, whose expectations are too easily met. We are content with mere passing pleasures when infinite joy is offered us.

Focus your energies. Processionary caterpillars may be content to march round and round till they die; but not you—not me. Life is only life when we risk all for a great cause.

Goals: Full Speed Ahead

Let's make a comparison. I once observed a race between two sailboats. From the looks of it, one boat was clearly superior—larger, sleeker, newer, the most advanced design, obviously more expensive. The other boat was far less distinctive; rather ordinary. As the race developed, I watched the gap widen between the boats. One slid through the water with remarkable speed. There was never a ripple in its sail. No ounce of wind was wasted. Its course was straight and true, and it won the race easily. The other ship's course was erratic, its efforts inefficient, and it settled for a distant second place.

The remarkable fact is that the winner was the ordinary-looking sailboat. The loser was the sleek, expensive craft.

The difference was the ability of the average boat's crew to chart a distinct course and to set and trim the sails in an efficient way.

The common element in all sailboats that win races is not their paint, their size, their color, their design. It is their course and the set of the sails.

Now for our comparison. As I grew up I had two friends who were also close friends to each other. One of them was exceptionally gifted—tall, handsome, athletic, an IQ close to the "genius" category, from a wealthy family. The other was average, toward the middle in his abilities. As we grew older, I watched the two go different directions. One excelled at literally everything he attempted. Today he is the exceptional father of a fine family, a success in business and financial affairs, a trusted leader in church and community. The other friend drifted, was content to just get by, settled for a life of mediocrity and frequent frustration. The remarkable thing is that the successful man today was my average friend. The mediocre, frustrated man was my gifted friend.

The thing that made my ordinary friend extraordinary was his well-conceived goals and his planning and tenacity in pursuing those goals. The second friend lacked this ability, and his gifts were wasted. The common element in all successful people is not their looks, their intelligence, their wealth. It is their ability to set and achieve goals. Without them, our hours, our days, our years are, to a large extent, wasted.

Have you ever had a day like Farmer Jones? Let's look at one of his days as recorded in his journal:

"Decided to cut the hay. Started to harness the horses, and found that a harness was broken; took it to the granary to repair it, and noticed some empty sacks; the sacks were a reminder that some potatoes in the cellar needed the sprouts removed; went to the cellar to do the job, and noticed the room needed sweeping; went to the house to get the broom and noticed the woodbox was empty; went to the woodpile, and noticed some ailing chickens. They were sad looking—poor things; decided to get some medicine for them. Out of medicine, so jumped in the car and headed for the drugstore. On the way, ran out of gas." (Author unidentified.)

How's that for going nowhere full speed ahead? That's what some of us do. We step on the gas as hard as we can and let go of the steering wheel. The result, in driving or in life, is the same. What a difference it makes to know where we're going, to have decided on the route, and *then* to step on the gas. Goals can do that for us.

It has been said that "the world turns aside for the man who knows where he is going." The tragedy is, few do. I am reminded of a visitor to my office, a young man in his early thirties. He wanted to be a success in life, to be a good husband and father, but he had seemed to encounter failure at every turn. I questioned him:

"What are some of your personal goals?"

"What goals do you and your wife have together?"

"What goals do you have as a family?"

His answer to all of these questions was revealing. He hadn't given it any thought.

With that interview in mind, may we, together, give goal setting some thought? Naturally, we can't delve deeply into all aspects of goal setting. But we can talk about some principles which we can apply now and which will make a difference in our lives.

First, and as a basis of all goal setting, know that you are a child of God; that life is eternal; that you will, upon death, return to him who made you to be judged and given rewards according to your life's work; that your Heavenly Father loves you and knows that you can succeed and, in fact, expects you to do so. Did Jesus not say, "Be ye therefore perfect"? Now, can you see how such a belief will affect your goals? It will make a positive difference. And it will avoid the problem described by an anonymous writer who said: "Some people reach the top rung of the ladder only to find it has been leaning against the wrong wall." The gospel of Jesus Christ helps us to put the ladder against the right wall.

Second, with a knowledge of the gospel and our relationship to our Heavenly Father in your minds and hearts, you are ready to set your goals. There need to be eternal goals, lifetime goals, intermediate goals, and short-term goals. What, after all, do you want in eternity?

1. To rejoin your Heavenly Father?

2. To live forever with your family?

What do you want out of life?

1. To raise a good family?

2. To have enough money to fill your needs?

What intermediate goals will you set to help you reach your righteous desires?

1. Spending meaningful time each day with each of your children?

2. Saving a little money in the bank each month?

And what will be your short-term goals?

1. Fulfilling a school assignment the best you've ever done?

2. Taking time to share a special experience you've had with a friend?

You know, it even makes a difference to take a piece of paper each morning and write down your goals for the day. Check them off as you complete them. And be sure you accomplish the ones that are really important. You will find that you will accomplish more. Your days will be more productive and enjoyable. And most important, those goals that seem so distant and hard to reach will begin to look not only possible, but also probable. You will find a new zest for life.

Now, may I give you a warning and a challenge? Setting and achieving goals will require great tenacity. You will get discouraged, but you can do it. Be positive! I know a young teenage golfer who set some pretty high goals for his golf game, even before he played his first game. During that "first-ever" round of golf, this young man came to the fifth hole—a par 4, 380-yard dogleg to the left. Well, after three shots, he was approximately 50 yards down the fairway. As he took his fourth shot (a tremendous dribbler of another 25 yards), he looked up at his companions and with great feeling hollered, "Shoot! There goes my par!" Well, you golfers will appreciate his position. But more importantly, you will appreciate his attitude. I have a feeling he will reach those goals he has set for himself. So be positive. Set your goals and go to work on them, and you will succeed. I know you will.

One final bit of advice. When reaching for worthy goals, there is a help available that will give you great power when all else fails. Your Heavenly Father will bless you in your efforts if you will but ask him. On one occasion a great young prophet said:

"I will go and do the things which the Lord hath commanded, for I know that the Lord giveth no commandments unto the children of men, save he shall prepare a way for them that they may accomplish the thing which he commandeth them." (1 Nephi 3:7.) Since the Lord has set the goal of perfection for each one of us, he will help us achieve that goal if we will ask him. And I bear testimony that he will bless us to achieve those daily, weekly, monthly, and lifetime goals which will help us do what he has asked. He is our Father. He cares.

Finally, I conclude with a quote from Tagore: "The song that I came to sing remains unsung. . . . I have spent my days in stringing and unstringing my instrument." Isn't that graphic? How many of God's children spend their lives stringing and unstringing their instruments—never really singing the song they were placed on earth to sing?

May that not be our destiny. I bear testimony that it won't be if we will set worthy goals and then work and persist. Be assured your Heavenly Father has placed you on earth for a purpose. You will find and achieve that purpose if you will set your goals and strive with diligence to reach them. You will be blessed to truly "sing your song." I know that to be true. And I bear you that testimony as I encourage us all to reach up to a Father who wants us to succeed.

On Making Resolutions

Have you ever felt like the man in this poem?

"Itch of haydust in the sweaty shirt and shoes.
Out in the hot corral—the old mare nosing lunch pails.
Grasshoppers crackling in the weeds.
I'm seventy-eight, he said.
I first bucked hay when I was seventeen.
I thought the day I started
I sure would hate to do this all my life.
And darn it, that's just what I've gone and done."

We're all so full of good resolutions, ideas to make us resounding successes. You know the kind I mean—tomorrow I'll start my diet; tomorrow I'll get up earlier; tomorrow I'll spend more time with my children. We think someday something will come along to suddenly make us change, to make our resolutions—once and for all—really effective.

Somehow we think we have unlimited time to become who we

want to be. If a resolve is broken, a desire dimmed, we think, "There's always tomorrow." But time has a way of running on—silent, illusive, unresting, and one day we find ourselves asking, as one grandmother always did when she looked in the mirror, "Who in the world is that old lady?"

The great question each of us has to determine is, "How do we keep the interest and the motivation secure enough to ultimately develop that which is ours?"

Our good resolves, so often broken, remind me of a home I once saw that was under construction. The house struck my fancy because it was almost identical to a plan that my wife had hoped we would one day build.

I found myself, more often than not, going that way on my way to work just to see the progress on the house that was not even mine. A month or two went by and the house was about two-thirds completed. Then one morning as I passed that way, I noticed that the workmen had ceased their labors. No work was being accomplished.

The days grew into weeks. The thing that gave me the most concern, as I'm sure it did the owner, was that the once bright, shiny new lumber was now starting to fade because it was not yet painted. It turned first to a light brown, then to a darker brown, and then to a kind of off-yellow, indicating that the deterioration process had set in.

Then one morning as I passed by to see if there had been any progress, one of the eternal truths of the New Testament came very forcefully to my mind. Luke tells about an incident in the life of the Savior when a great multitude gathered and, as they frequently did, commenced to ask questions in an attempt to trap him. In this setting, the Savior said something profound which applies to the rotting house and to all of us with broken resolves.

"For which of you, intending to build a tower, sitteth not down first, and counteth the cost, whether he have sufficient to finish it?

"Lest haply, after he hath laid the foundation, and is not able to finish it, all that behold it begin to mock him,

"Saying, this man began to build, and was not able to finish.

"Or what king, going to make war against another king, sitteth not down first, and consulteth whether he be able with ten thousand to meet him that cometh against him with twenty thousand?'' (Luke 14:28-31.)

Everything we want to become, every talent we want to shine, will cost us something. A wish never was a win. Count the cost behind your good resolves. How many would-be pianists are there who started lessons and weren't willing to stick out the long hours of practice between ''Chopsticks'' and Chopin?

If we are discontented with our lives, it isn't because we have too much desire for too many things. It is because we have too little desire. We don't want what we want with enough passion, stamina, or courage. We don't want what we want enough to propel us past discouragement, disappointment, or dragging days.

There are many formulas for success, but none of them work unless you do.

A famous lawyer said it this way: ''When I hear congratulations tendered to a man on his 'luck' in achieving a success, or when I am greeted in a similar fashion after a courtroom victory, I am inclined to recall that this type of 'luck' usually visits me at 2:00 A.M. on a cold morning when, red-eyed and bone-weary, I am poring over law books, preparing a case. It never visits me when I'm at the movies, when I'm on a golf course, or when I'm reclining in an easy chair.''

Everyone of us has to realize this simple truth: No one can realize my possibilities for me but *me*. No one can fly me to my dream. I have to walk there step by step. The secret to making successful resolves is not luck. It is unvanquished desire, untiring energy, and unremitting concentration. It is counting the cost of your dream, deciding if you are equal to it, then working even when you are weary.

The museum in Italy that houses Michelangelo's masterpiece, the *David,* is also filled with his unfinished pieces—the products of his lagging days. As one walks down the aisle one sees blocks of stone with a leg sticking out here, an arm there. Each of them was started with great hope but was left in despair. And then at the end of this aisle of apparent defeat stands the *David*—every muscle, every angle so exquisite in its beauty, such a monument to the genius of its creator.

Never give up that vision of yourself, that dream of who you might be. The Lord placed that divine discontent in you that calls you to be more than you are, that keeps you making resolutions and dreaming dreams. With all the yearning of your soul, begin your quest for excellence today.

May I suggest ten principles that you might want to consider in your quest for excellence.

1. People will continue to go where invited and remain where appreciated.

2. Reputations will continue to be made by many acts, and lost by one.

3. People will go right on preferring to do business with friends.

4. Go-givers will become the best go-getters.

5. The extra mile will have no traffic jams.

6. Performance will continue to outsell promises.

7. Enthusiasm will remain as contagious as ever.

8. Know-how will surpass guess-how.

9. Trust, not tricks, will keep friends loyal.

10. Quality will be prized as a precious possession.

Work

Recently I was engaged in a conversation with a group of young people concerning the philosophy of hedonism—the idea that pleasure is the chief good in life. It was an interesting discussion, to say the least. One young man quoted an economist of a prestigious businessmen's organization who said, "The most that can be said for work is that it is an unfortunate necessity."

Now, that's quite a statement. No wonder work is fighting a difficult battle to be included among life's virtues.

Contrast the statement of our businessman with one made by the Lord to Father Adam. The statement was made to earth's first couple as they were about to be driven out into the lone and dreary world. Said the Lord: ". . . cursed is the ground *for thy sake*. . . ." (Genesis 3:17; italics added.)

That's interesting! The Lord had just indicated that because of Adam's choice he would be compelled to work by "the sweat of thy face" (Genesis 3:19), and, at the same time, our earthly brother was told that it was all being done "for thy sake." It reminds me of the father who, while spanking his young son, reminded the boy that he was doing it because he loved him—whereupon the lad indicated his desire to grow rapidly so that he could soon return his father's love!

But the Lord *does* love us. And what seems to us sometimes to be "cruel and unusual punishment" (work) can be our greatest blessing. Calvin Coolidge expressed it beautifully:

"All growth depends upon activity. There is no development physically or intellectually without effort, and effort means work. Work is not a curse; it is the prerogative of intelligence, the only means to manhood, and the measure of civilization." That statement carries such deep importance that it could be re-read by us all every day. Work *is* a blessing; it's a key to happiness and success. Dr. William Osler put it in a different way:

"Though little, the master word looms large in meaning. It is the 'open sesame' to every portal, the great equalizer, the philosopher's stone which transmutes all base metal of humanity into gold. The stupid it will make bright, the bright brilliant, and the brilliant steady. To youth it brings hope, to the middle-aged confidence, to the aged repose. . . . Not only has it been the touchstone of progress, but it is the measure of success in everyday life. And the master word is *work*."

Although President Abraham Lincoln never read that quote, he knew what it meant. His taking pains with a job became somewhat akin to genius in its effect. He was once invited to "make a few appropriate remarks" at the dedication of the Gettysburg National Cemetery. President Lincoln's hard work and desire for excellence resulted in an address of only 265 words. But instead of the "usual," he produced something beautiful and of lasting value.

The other day I read an interesting definition of work. It went something like this:

"Work is some purposeful activity that requires the expenditure of energy with some sacrifice of leisure."

How about that? Purposeful activity, expenditure of energy, and sacrifice of leisure are all required. And yet, without a willingness to do any of these three, people will be heard to say, "I want my life to mean something!" Your life *can* mean something if you will pay the price, if you will work. A prophet of God emphasized that point when he said: "I assert with confidence that the law of success, here and hereafter, is to have a humble and a prayerful heart, and to work, *work*, WORK." (President Heber J. Grant, *Improvement Era*, 3 (January 1900): 195.) The sooner we learn how important work is to our happiness and success, the better off we will be. Talent and ability alone will not do it.

But ability, however limited, combined with hard work and enthusiasm will do the job. Let me share a true experience. I grew up in the grocery business. At one time I became a manager of a new supermarket in Southern California. One afternoon I got a call from a sixteen-year-old high school boy. He was very much to the point, very polite, and radiated just enough self-confidence that I wanted to listen for a moment. He used the right terminology—he always said "yes, sir" and let me take the lead.

The young man said, "Mr. Dunn, you don't know me, but I have watched with great interest the opening of your fine market in our community. My mother has been a constant shopper there ever since, and she is delighted!"

I don't know how delighted she really was, but I was ready to hear more.

He said, "I realize that you probably have all of your positions filled, but I believe I have something that will help your business. At a time that is convenient to you, sir, I would like to present my credentials. May I?" A sixteen-year-old boy!

I wanted to hear more about him. I said, "How about Wednesday afternoon after school?"

"Yes, sir, I'll be there." So we set an appointment for four o'clock.

At one minute to four, here came this young man, properly dressed and with a certain amount of confidence in his walk. I am sure he was scared to death. He probably had more butterflies than most of us have as he approached this interview.

As we walked into the office, I had him take a seat. I pulled up a chair beside him and said, "Tell me just a little bit about yourself."

He said, "I have had experience as a box boy on Saturdays. I believe I know enough of the business to be an asset to your organization. I don't expect you to believe that, but, because I do have some ability, I'd like to prove it to you. May we step out into the store for just a moment?''

I said, ''Why, certainly.''

So we did, and he took me over to the wall where all the canned goods were lined up. In opening the store we were having a difficult time keeping the shelves properly stocked.

He said, ''Now, Mr. Dunn, I think you know enough about sales appeal and the intuition of women as they shop around in a store to realize that if that shelf could always look full and properly aligned, you could probably increase your sales. I'm the greatest boy in the world in terms of keeping shelves stocked. I don't expect you to believe that either. You even look a little doubtful, but would you be willing to let me invest one week of my time every afternoon after school and all day Saturday to show you what I can do? And you have no obligation, sir.''

What do you imagine I was thinking? At that time I had five part-time box boys, and they were all the ''let's-see-what-time-we-can-get-out-of-here'' boys. These kids would always gather at the counter with their friends. They were more concerned about acceptance with their peer group than they were about what they could give to a business. They had capacity, but they lacked the will to serve through hard work.

Now if you were managing a store, which element would you want? Do I have to tell you what I did? I had him take his coat off and show me. He worked that one afternoon, and I didn't need to watch him very long. I let three boys go the next Saturday, because this young man could fill all three positions.

Was the opportunity there? Maybe it wasn't obvious, but he created one. He had the ability, but more important he had the will to work hard.

Who do you think got the consistent raises? Who do you think I made openings for in the future as the store volume dropped and settled to normal? Who do you think was going to succeed in college? Who do you think was going to the top in business with an attitude like this? There is no question!

That young man reminds me of Tamerlane, the celebrated warrior. He once learned a great lesson in hard work and perseverance from an insect. When being hotly pursued by his enemies, Tamerlane took refuge in some old ruins. There, left alone, he spied an ant tugging and working to carry a single grain of corn. His efforts were repeated sixty-nine times, but each time he fell back with his burden. Then, on the seventieth time, the ant bore away his prize in triumph. What a lesson about work and its rewards!

The author of the following lines, whose identity I do not know, had learned how honest labor can lift our lives to a higher plane:

Work

"Work brings man to life, sets him in motion. Work is man in action doing things. Nothing happens until people go to work. Work creates the world we live in.

"The art of work consists of what you think about your work, how you feel about your work and what you do about your work.

"It is abolishing the concept of work as chains and slavery, and seeing it as freedom to create and help build.

"It is striving to find work you can love, a job to which you can harness your heart.

"It is idealizing your work, turning a job into a mission, a task into a career.

"It is doing your present work so well that it will open doors to new opportunities. Tasks done at a high standard pave the way to bigger things.

"It is discovering the great healing power of work. If you are lonely, *work!* If you are worried or fearful, *work!* If you are discouraged or defeated, *work!* Work is the key to happiness.

"It is making your work *you*. It is putting the stamp of your unique personality on the work you do. It is pouring your spirit into your task. It is making your work a reflection of your faith, your integrity, your ideals.

"It is recognizing that work, not repose, is the destiny of man.

"James W. Elliot said it all in nine words: 'Work is life, and good work is good life.' "

I would remind us all that, since life is eternal, and I bear testimony that it is, we should learn the joy of work now so that we can enjoy it forever. Eternal progression is eternal work—but work in the most noble sense of the word. If we want to be successful, if we want to be happy, we must work. There is no other way.

Remember our definition of work? Purposeful activity, expenditure of energy, sacrifice of time. I challenge us all to learn how to do those three things and to do them well. The effort will be rewarded now and forever. May we receive both the counsel and the blessing of the Lord when he said to Solomon, and to us: "Arise therefore, and be doing, and the Lord be with thee." (1 Chronicles 22:16.)

Becoming a Success

Have you ever felt like just giving up on your dreams? As if all the things you always thought you'd be could never come to pass? Have you ever come to that dull day when the vision of what your life would hold has slipped and you settled for something less than you wanted?

There is a little rhyme by Whittier that goes,

> "Of all sad words of tongue or pen
> The saddest are these: It might have been."

It might have been—those are words that can haunt your soul as you see all the possibilities the world holds out, for the truth is simple but profound: you'll never be fully happy until you become who you were meant to be—an accomplished, fulfilled, blazing success. There is promise in your soul beyond your wildest imaginings, and if in despair or disappointment you've given up on yourself, you've given up more than you dream.

Have you ever heard the parable of the eagle? A certain man went through the forest seeking any bird of interest he might find.

He caught a young eagle, brought it home, and put it among his fowls and ducks and turkeys and gave it chicken's food to eat even though it was an eagle, the king of the birds.

Five years later a naturalist came to see him and, after passing through his garden, said, "That bird is an eagle, not a chicken."

"Yes," said its owner. "But I have trained it to be a chicken. It is no longer an eagle. It is a chicken, even though it measures fifteen feet from tip to tip of its wings."

"No," said the naturalist. "It is an eagle still; it has the heart of an eagle, and I will make it soar high up to the heavens."

"No," said the owner. "It is a chicken, and it will never fly."

They agreed to test it. The naturalist picked up the eagle and said to it, "Thou dost belong to the sky and not to this earth; stretch forth thy wings and fly." The eagle turned this way and that and then, looking down, saw the chickens eating their food, and down he jumped.

The owner said, "I told you it was a chicken."

"No," said the naturalist. "It is an eagle. Give it another chance tomorrow."

So the next day he took it to the top of the house and said, "Eagle, thou art an eagle; stretch forth thy wings and fly." But again the eagle, seeing the chickens feeding, jumped down and fed with them.

Then the owner said, "I told you it was a chicken."

"No," asserted the naturalist. "It is an eagle, and it still has the heart of an eagle. Only give it one more chance, and I will make it fly tomorrow."

The next morning he rose early and took the eagle outside the city, away from the houses to the foot of a high mountain. The sun was just rising, gilding the top of the mountain with gold, and every crag was glistening in the joy of that beautiful morning.

He picked up the eagle and said to it, "Eagle, thou art an eagle. Thou dost belong to the sky and not to this earth. Stretch forth thy wings and fly." The eagle looked around and trembled as if new life were coming to it. But it did not fly. The naturalist then made it look straight at the sun. Suddenly it stretched out its wings and, with the screech of an eagle, flew.

For all of you who are keeping your eyes cast down with the chickens, for you who are grubbing and pecking like a chicken because you doubt your ability to succeed at your dearest dream, remember the words: "O eagle, thou art an eagle. Thou dost belong to the sky and not to this earth. Stretch forth thy wings and fly."

Do you doubt it? Do you question that you have more ability, more intelligence, more drive than you even begin to give yourself credit for?

Here is what a theologian, Parley P. Pratt, had to say about it: "An intelligent being in the image of God possesses every organ, attribute, sense, sympathy, affection that is possessed by God himself. But these are possessed by man in his rudimental state, in the subordinate sense of the word. Or in other words, these attributes are in embryo and are to be gradually developed. They resemble a bud, a germ, which gradually develops into bloom, and then, by progress, produces fruit after its own kind."

Can you even imagine that? Within that being of yours, no matter what failings you have (and you probably know those all too well), is every attribute possessed by God, every quality just waiting to be developed.

C. S. Lewis, the famous English theologian, said it another way:

"It is a serious thing to live in a society of possible gods and goddesses, to remember that the dullest and most uninteresting person you talk to may one day be a creature which you would be strongly tempted to worship, or else a horror and a corruption such as you now meet, if at all, only in a nightmare. All day long we are in some degree helping each other to one or the other of these destinations. There are no ordinary people. You have never talked to a mere mortal. Nations, cultures, arts, civilizations—these are mortal, and their life is to ours as the life of a gnat. But it is immortals whom we joke with, work with, marry, snub and exploit—immortal horrors or everlasting splendors."

Look around to the immortals passing by you every day. Look inside to the possibilities hiding there. Becoming a success? You have everything it takes to be something special in this world.

Even psychologists, scholars who may refute that there is a

Supreme Being, say that man has not begun to plumb his potential. Most of us use but a tiny percentage of that lovely brain in our heads. How many languages could we speak? What great poetry could we write? What scientific insight could we proclaim if we could but call on the power in our own heads?

What we need is to be filled with a divine discontent, a reaching, a stretching, an aching to be what we can be, to belong to the sky. We need to recognize that the deepest urge of our being is to use our powers, to develop our gifts. All of us have an innate need to shine in use, a desire to increase the bounds of ourselves, to learn more, do more, express more, a desire to grow, improve, accomplish, expand. It's an energy that originates from our deepest being.

When you feel most like quitting, dust off your dreams and remember this Scottish prayer: "Oh God, help me to hold a high opinion of myself."

You have every reason to.

Dare
to Try

William Shakespeare gave us some great wisdom and excellent counsel. Perhaps none was greater than when he said,

>   ". . . Our doubts are traitors
> And make us lose the good we oft might win
>   By fearing to attempt. . . ."

Let me repeat that one more time: "Our doubts are traitors and make us lose the good we oft might win by fearing to attempt." I think most failures are not due to a lack of opportunity but rather to unwillingness to "think big." Sometimes we just do not *dare to try!*

I recall a group of teenage youth in Uruguay who, more out of nerve than talent, entered a certain soccer tournament. What they lacked in ability they made up for in sheer determination. They had practiced together long and hard and somehow or other they managed to make it to the championship game. They were obviously outclassed by the defending champions. Unfortunately, someone told them about it and they believed it. At the end of the first half the score stood 4 to 0. They were zero—in more ways than one.

Their coach pulled them aside during the halftime. He kept it simple. "Look, you guys, I know what you're against. I know those guys have talent. But I know you, and let me tell you something. I know you can still win this thing if you really want to. I'm only ashamed because you haven't tried. All I ask is that you go out there and give it your all. I know you guys well enough to know you have what it takes. *Now go do it!*"

And they did!—5 to 4, scoring the final goal in the closing seconds of play as bedlam erupted in the stands. Those young men learned a lesson that will last them a long time.

I recall a young man in Los Angeles who wanted to be an operatic star. Several teachers told him that it would do him no good to try because, they said, "you just don't have the voice." But, unwilling to give up, he finally discovered one teacher who saw the value of his hidden talent and big determination. Today, after years of conscientious, careful direction of his power toward a single goal, he is one of the most pleasing and highly honored singers on the West Coast.

Did you know that Verdi, the composer of some of our finest grand operas, was at one time refused admission to a music conservatory because of his apparent lack of natural ability? And that a prominent music teacher once refused to take Caruso as a student because he could see in Caruso's voice no promise in the musical world?

Just like those young soccer players in Uruguay, it's not so much a matter of talent as it is determination and willingness to try—to think big. As one good wife reminded her husband on a note taped to his bathroom mirror:

"It doesn't take a muscle spasm
To show a little enthusiasm."

When I wanted to be a ball player some years ago, a great high school coach taught me a principle. When I went in to sign up as a freshman, he asked, "Do you want to be a ball player or a champion?"

I replied, "I want to play ball."

He said: "If you just want to play ball, then you won't play here. But if you want to be a champion, you came to the right place because I make champions, and a champion you will be." Isn't that a great thought!

Now if you think back with me for a moment on the previous stories I have related, you will notice a couple of common denominators running through each of them. Once there was a vision of what could be accomplished and an attitude of "I can do it," another critical commitment was made. Besides a willingness to try came the consciousness and determination to pay the necessary price.

Some of us, however, being mortals, are willing to consider the cost and make the commitment but just can't seem to follow through. If you're willing to put what we're talking about to the test, you will find that the Savior was serious when he said:

"There is a law, irrevocably decreed in heaven before the foundations of this world, upon which all blessings are predicated—

"And when we obtain any blessing from God, it is by obedience to that law upon which it is predicated." (D&C 130:20-21.)

The Savior means it! If you're willing to pay the price and do what is necessary, in righteousness, you will certainly reap the reward.

Given an average grade of intelligence, wise direction, and willingness to pay the price of concentrated and consecrated effort—not once a week but constantly, every day of every year—we will find that the secrets of life have a way of yielding themselves beyond our fondest dreams. Most of us know of many cases of particular individuals who years ago were just average or less but who were not satisfied with mediocrity or the average, and who today exhibit great personal talent. By aligning themselves with great causes, seeking out people who are geniuses in their fields, and training and disciplining themselves, they have gone on to make tremendous contributions to themselves and to society.

Just remember that there will be times of discouragement. But in such times I would encourage you to remember the words of a great coach: "Just remember that when you see a man on top of a mountain he didn't fall there." Success and greatness are processes of climbing, and climb we must.

Life can be exciting! Each one of us should dream—we should

think big—we should dare to try. It has been my experience that those who are truly happy in life are those who do! You or I can be one of those. The Savior of this world has promised his help if we seek it—if our dreams are worthy—if our efforts are to bless those around us. I challenge you—I challenge you to dare to try!

Just for Today

I had a friend in college whose chief purpose was to study, so he gathered all the needed equipment. He procured a large, comfortable chair that was thought to be good for study. He got study slippers and a lounging jacket. A bookrest was fastened to the arm of the chair to hold the book at the right angle before his eyes. A special lamp and a revolving bookcase were installed, and an eyeshade, pencils, and paper were provided. He would come into the room after the evening meal, take off his coat and put on the jacket, take off his shoes and slip into the slippers, adjust the study lamp, put his book on the bookrest, recline in the comfortable chair with his eyeshade over his eyes, and when everything was perfectly adjusted, he would go to sleep.

Do you ever wonder where your life goes? Have you ever heard people say:

Life sure passed me by!

or

I can't believe how time flies!

or

I just can't find time!

or

There are not enough hours in the day!

Sound familiar? It seems to me all of us have said something like that at one time or another. In fact, in our fast-moving world those statements are made more and more often. Statisticians tell us that if we live to be seventy and lead an ''average life'' we'll spend

13 years gaining an education
8 years at the dinner table
5 years in traveling
4 years in conversation (perhaps a
little longer for the fairer sex!)
14 years in work
3 years in reading
24 years in sleeping

That seems pretty cut and dried. But I wonder. Anyway, here's a good question: How is it some of our fellow travelers find time not only to dream but to make their dreams come true?

In *The Wizard of Oz,* those plaintive last lines Dorothy sings have been sung by the human family since our Eternal Father placed us here: ''Why, then, oh, why can't I?'' Of course, there's a myriad of reasons why we don't—and an equal number of solutions to the problem. But after all's said and done, a great part of the reason we don't and a great part of the solution to the problem is simply the element of *time*. Somehow we aren't always willing to pay the price in time.

Let's take an example: Remember the average life of seventy years? Suppose a young man or woman seeks a close and personal relationship with his Father in heaven—that's his dream! Well, if he goes to church every week and prays five minutes each morning and night, he will be giving fifteen months to God! Fifteen months out of a life of seventy years! Is that enough? Will his dream be realized by spending fifteen months' worth of his time? Isn't there more to it than that?

How about a father and mother whose dream and goal in life is to be good parents, to be close to their children? Is that a realistic dream? I believe it is. What it takes is good common sense and time. Kids love parents who, from the beginning, are willing to spend time with them. A nighttime story takes five minutes. Helping with homework may take a half-hour (except for new math!). Sincerely listening to a teenager's problem may take a few minutes each day. An outing together may take two hours. Working in the yard together may take half a day a week. Going on vacation together may take two weeks a year. But it all adds up. And where time is ungrudgingly given, dreams come true.

Even though "time flies on wings of lightning," we can certainly determine the direction it takes.

Ellis Shipp is a little-known but fascinating pioneer woman. She was married at the age of nineteen to Milford Shipp. Nine days after her third son was born, her husband was called on a two-year mission to Europe. Ellis supported her little family with no more than a cow, an orchard, and a garden plot. She sewed and knitted and took in a student boarder, but she was not satisfied with her ability to care for and educate her children. She had had only one year of formal schooling, so she developed a plan of study, arising every morning at 4:00 A.M. so she could put in three solid hours of study each day before her husband returned from his mission. Various entries in her diary tell of her early-morning program of studying poetry, history, English grammar, hygiene, and health. She became Utah's first woman doctor.

Imagine getting up every morning at 4:00 A.M. Time can really make a difference, and the great thing about time is that we generally have as much of it as anybody else. It's up to us.

I have a friend who is a doctor. He's a heart specialist and one of the best in the world. He's paid the price to become that kind of doctor. But do you know the best thing about my friend? He still has taken time to become a great husband and father. He also uses his time to be a civic leader. And he somehow finds time to hold a responsible position in the Church.

I have another young friend who is using part of his time to accomplish his dream of becoming a great lawyer. His family doesn't even have to nag to get him to night school. And so the story goes — on and on — as people use this priceless commodity to fulfill their dreams.

Now, I've saved the best for last. I would imagine an overriding dream of us all is to be happy. Sometimes we aren't sure how to do that, but that's what we want. We have a loving Father in heaven who also wants us to be happy. In fact, he once said, through a prophet, "Men are, that they might have joy." (2 Nephi 2:25.) He cares what happens to us and does as much for us as we'll let him do. He wants us to be happy now and return to him and be happy in his presence forever. But everything depends on how we use our time. There are a couple of simple things we can do to make sure we use our time wisely. We can:

1. Make sure our "dreams" are worthy of our time and effort.

2. Get busy and spend the time necessary to fulfill them.

It's a little like avoiding the attitude of the man who once said: "I think I'm undecided, but I'm not sure."

The Lord will bless us as we strive to use the precious gift of time on things that will bring us and others happiness now and eternally. Will you accept this challenge:

Just for Today

"Just for today I will try to live through this day only, not tackle my whole life problem at once. I can do things for twelve hours that would appall me if I had to keep them up for a lifetime.

"Just for today I will be happy. This assumes that what Abraham Lincoln said is true that 'Most folks are about as happy as they make up their minds to be.' Happiness is from within; it is not a matter of externals.

"Just for today I will try to adjust myself to what is and not try to adjust everything to my own desires. I will take my family, my business, and my luck as they come and fit myself to them.

"Just for today I will take care of my body. I will exercise it, care for it, nourish it, and not abuse it or neglect it so that it will be a perfect machine for my bidding.

"Just for today I will try to strengthen my mind. I will learn something useful. I will not be a mental loafer. I will read something that requires effort, thought, and concentration.

"Just for today I will exercise my soul in these ways: I will do somebody a good turn and not get found out. I will do at least two things I don't want to do, as William James suggests, just for exercise.

"Just for today I will be agreeable. I will look as well as I can, dress as becomingly as possible, talk low, act courteously, be liberal with praise, criticize not at all, nor find fault with anything, and not try to regulate or improve anyone.

"Just for today I will have a quiet half hour all by myself and relax. In this half hour sometimes I will think of God, so as to get a little more perspective to my life."

The Game
of Life

In paradise there was to be a big baseball game between the hosts of heaven and the forces below. The two coaches got together, and one, a heavenly messenger, said to one of the imps of the adversary, "Do you realize what you're asking?"

The imp said, "I think so."

The heavenly messenger said, "You recognize, of course, that in heaven we can field a varsity team of former hall-of-famers."

"Yes," the little imp said, "but you ought to understand that we have all the umpires."

Well, it's that season for spring training, time to get those tired winter muscles working again. And from the looks of it, Americans are taking that task seriously. Jogging, for instance, makes many of our hearts beat faster. In fact, *The Complete Book of Running* has been on the best-seller list for many weeks. Joggers come in all shapes and sizes. There are young girls, middle-aged executives, one-legged hobblers and even one eighty-seven-year-old woman with heart trouble. No rocking and knitting for her.

As I've watched the Boston marathon grow bigger each year, as I've strained in sympathy as the large assortment of runners come huffing and puffing into the finish line at our local marathon, I've wondered—what is the mystery that makes someone jog? Why would an otherwise normal human being run until his side aches and his legs feel like rubber and his breath comes like sharp knives into his lungs?

I heard one physician say that there had been arguments on both sides as to whether jogging helped the heart. But as for him, he didn't care if he had a heart attack and died while jogging, it was still worth it.

What's the secret that keeps America jogging? Why do we play baseball and football, squash and tennis? Why are we willing to exercise or jump the rope until it hurts?

I think it has something to do with the vigor we feel when we push ourselves toward something grand. It has something to do with the glory of the private victory when spirit triumphs over flesh. Society today would have us believe the ultimate life is one of self-indulgence. But the ultimate life for anyone really human is one of self-discipline, finding that divine spark that keeps us running and trying when everything about us shouts, "Give up!"

Do you remember when Roger Bannister ran the first four-minute mile? He had been disappointed at his performance in the 1952 Olympics and had just about decided to give up running. But his coach told him to give it one more chance. So Bannister, a medical student with ten hours a day of studying, decided to break that four-minute barrier before he quit running. He worked out for months for four hours a day, and then the big race came.

The fourth lap of the race was the hard one. As he rounded the last turn, his head throbbed and his lungs seemed ready to burst. He began to say to himself, "Slacken up, and just try for a win." But then another voice welled up inside of him and said, "Roger, if you run until you collapse on this track, you are going to make this four-minute mile. If your knees hit this track you are going to do it. For all these months you have trained, and you've got to." So instead of slackening the pace, he fought off the pain, picked up his legs, and began sprinting. The rest is history. He turned in a time of

3 minutes 59.4 seconds. Roger Bannister had broken through the "impossible" four-minute-mile barrier.

Maybe it's this kind of self-discipline, this vigorous self-denial, this blazing beyond mere amusement so evident in fine athletes that urged the apostle Paul to use athletic images in so many of his letters. Paul perceived in sports one of the greatest things that training can offer: the will to win. As he wrote to the Corinthians: "Know ye not that they which run in a race run all, but one receiveth the prize? So run, that ye may obtain." (1 Corinthians 9:24.)

Paul had seen the great Greek games held every two years at Corinth. To participate in the footracing, boxing, jumping, wrestling, and javelin and discus throwing, a person had to face months, even years, of rigorous training and long practice. The prize for this self-discipline was a mere wreath or crown of pine twigs, of ivy leaves, but a winner was welcomed in his native city with great honor.

Now, if a crown of ivy is worth such sustained effort and total dedication, Paul told the early Christian converts, with how much more vigor and zeal should we strive for the crown of righteousness. Every athlete, he said, exercises self-control in all things. He does it to receive a perishable wreath—just a simple little twig—but we, an imperishable one. Paul told his friend Timothy: "I have fought a good fight, I have finished my course, I have kept the faith: Henceforth there is laid up for me a crown of righteousness, which the Lord, the righteous judge, shall give me at that day." (2 Timothy 4:7-8.)

And then again to Timothy, Paul gave this great admonition. An athlete is not crowned unless he competes according to the rules. (See 2 Timothy 2:5.) There's a great sermon in a single line for this "do your own thing" generation.

What would tennis be like without the net? Imagine basketball without the hoop or golf without the sand traps. What's the fun of racing without a standard to match and beat?

Life, like sports, is made up of interesting rules and regulations, and one can become the victor only as he competes according to the standards of the game. Some of us have a hard time occasionally discerning why any rules should apply to us. But just as a game or an athletic competition loses its zest and flavor when we don't play according to the rules, so does life.

Dishonesty in business. Just getting by on assignments given to us. Putting up false appearances. Abortion. Sometimes we think self-indulgence will make us happy. We bend and break our moral standards in the search for pleasure. If an athlete played a game that way, he'd never make the team.

My high school coach had each boy on his team sign a contract saying he would obey certain rules and regulations, including a health code. He said: "Now, if you're going to play ball for me, you'll play according to the rules. Is that understood?"

Well, as he was giving his pep talk, our all-star second baseman was standing in the circle with his hands on his hips. When the coach passed him by, he stopped and did a double-take. "Jimmy," he said, "is that a nicotine stain on your finger?"

He said, "Yes, sir."

The coach said, "Well, don't you know the rule?"

"Well . . . yes, sir."

"Did you sign a contract with me?"

"Yes, sir."

The coach said: "You've lost your privilege. Turn in your uniform."

I almost shouted (but I didn't), "Coach, wait till tomorrow. We've got a game."

Jimmy was batting .380 and as a second baseman had not made an error in league play. And he now had to turn in his uniform.

The next day I drew the assignment to pitch. The game went into extra innings, and they beat us one to nothing in the top of the thirteenth. Do you know how it happened? A ground ball was hit to second, and the ball went through the substitute's legs, and that proved to be the winning run. I went home that night and literally cried myself to sleep.

That was over twenty years ago, and I thank God this day for a great man who taught me that you have to play according to standards or you can't really win.

Our life is a race, a game, greater than any mere athletic event.

It's worth giving it everything we've got to live up to standards of righteousness and finish with the crown of honor and eternal life.

The apostle Paul watched as the marathon runners in the Greek games went up and laid aside their armor to race. In them he saw this great vision of life: "Let us lay aside every weight, and the sin which doth so easily beset us, and let us run with patience the race that is set before us, Looking unto Jesus the author and finisher of our faith." (Hebrews 12:1-2.)

God bless us to run the great race with faith, confidence, and the desire to finish.

The Wonder
of Learning

A humorous college boy bought his grandmother a special present for her eightieth birthday. It was a beautiful, leatherbound, gilt-edged Bible. The note he left inside simply said this: ''I thought you might need some help cramming for finals.''

Well, college boys ought to know something about cramming for finals. And I wonder how many of us have crammed for our last school tests, collected our diplomas, and called our education finished. If we have, we've missed the most marvelous, turbulent, exotic adventure of them all—the adventure of the mind.

In a time when Americans are feverishly pursuing entertainment, when we have an extraordinary variety of diversions, psychiatrists estimate that as many as 20 percent of all Americans are handicapped by boredom.

We're bored, paralyzed, depressed. We have a passive, expectant attitude, hoping that the external world will supply the satisfaction missing in our lives. We turn thirty and say, ''I've done it all.'' ''There's nothing new under the sun.'' Idle ghetto youths vandalize buildings; bored adults turn a switch or swallow a pill and then wonder why life seems so flat and tasteless.

I've always liked the advice wise Merlin gave to King Arthur when the king was feeling low. "The best thing for being sad," said Merlin, beginning to puff and blow, "is to learn something. That is the only thing that never fails. You may grow old and trembling in your anatomies; you may lie awake at night listening to the disorder of your veins; you may miss your only love; you may see the world about you devastated by evil lunatics, or know your honor trampled in the sewers of baser minds. There is only one thing for it, then—to learn. Learn why the world wags and what wags it. That is the only thing which the mind can never exhaust, never alienate, never be tortured by, never fear or distrust, and never dream of regretting. Learning is the thing for you. Look at what a lot of things there are to learn—pure science, the only purity there is. You can learn astronomy in a lifetime, natural history in three, literature in six, and then, after you have exhausted a million lifetimes in biology and medicine and theocriticism and geography and history and economics, why, you can start to make a cartwheel out of the appropriate wood or spend fifty years learning to begin to beat your adversary at fencing. After that, you can start again on mathematics until it is time to learn to plow."

Merlin was a smart magician. How little any of us really know—even if we spend every waking hour of our lives expanding our minds. Who can fathom the reaches of the universe? Who understands the instinct of a salmon propelling it to swim thousands of miles back to its birthplace to spawn? Who comprehends how a fertilized egg divides and differentiates and becomes a human being?

Do you know that there is a shrub in the forest that will not germinate—that will grow hundreds, even thousands, of years without producing a seed—until a fire blazes through the woods?

Do you know that Leonardo da Vinci wrote in his notebook from right to left and backwards so that it could be read only in a mirror?

Do you know that the male bees, the drones, were mysteriously pushed out of the beehives early last year on the East Coast, predicting a hard winter?

Do you know that if a twin were sent from earth on a spaceship traveling the speed of light, when he returned home he would be years younger than his earthbound twin brother?

Our own surroundings offer us fascination, awe.

I like this story about a famous scholar. One night in London, at the conclusion of a lecture by the distinguished naturalist Dr. Louis Agassiz, a woman complained to him that she "had never had a chance." In response to her complaint, he replied: "Do you say, madam, you never had a chance? What do you do?"

"I am single and help my sister run a boardinghouse."

"What do you do?" he asked.

"I skin potatoes and chop onions."

He said, "Madam, where do you sit during these interesting but homely duties?"

"On the bottom step of the kitchen stairs."

"Where do your feet rest?"

"On the glazed brick."

"What is glazed brick?"

"I don't know, sir."

He said, "How long have you been sitting there?"

She said, "Fifteen years."

"Madam, here is my personal card," said Dr. Agassiz. "Would you kindly write me a letter concerning the nature of a glazed brick?"

She took him seriously. She went home and explored the dictionary and discovered that a brick was a piece of baked clay. That definition seemed too simple to send to Dr. Agassiz, so after the dishes were washed, she went to the library and in an encyclopedia read that a glazed brick is vitrified kaolin and hydrous aluminum silicate. She didn't know what that meant, but she was curious and found out. She took the word *vitrified* and read all she could find about it. Then she visited museums. She moved out of the basement of her life and into a new world on the wings of *vitrified*. And having started, she took the word *hydrous,* studied geology, and went back in her studies to the time when God started the world and laid the clay beds. One afternoon she went to a brickyard, where she found the history of more than 120 kinds of bricks and tiles, and why there have to be so many. Then she sat down and wrote thirty-six pages on the subject of glazed brick and tile.

Back came the letter from Dr. Agassiz: "Dear Madam, this is the best article I have ever seen on the subject. If you will kindly change the three words marked with asterisks I will have it published and pay you for it."

A short time later there came a letter that brought $250, and penciled on the bottom of this letter was this query: "What was under those bricks?" She had learned the value of time and answered with a single word: "Ants." He wrote back and said, "Tell me about the ants."

She began to study ants. She found there were between eighteen hundred and twenty-five hundred different kinds. There are ants so tiny you could put three head-to-head on a pin and have standing room left over for other ants; ants an inch long that march in solid armies half a mile wide, driving everything ahead of them; ants that are blind; ants that get wings on the afternoon of the day they die; ants that build anthills so tiny that you can cover one with a lady's silver thimble; peasant ants that keep cows to milk, and then deliver the fresh milk to the apartment house of the aristocratic ants of the neighborhood.

After wide reading, much microscopic work, and deep study, the spinster sat down and wrote Dr. Agassiz 360 pages on the subject. He published the book and sent her the money, and she went to visit all the lands of her dreams on the proceeds of her work. (Story from Marion D. Hanks, *The Gift of Self* (Bookcraft, Inc., 1974), pp. 151-153.)

"I never had a chance." "My life offers me nothing." The best antidote for the "blahs" is to take William Blake's advice and "see a world in a grain of sand, and a heaven in a wild flower."

Learn. Find out. Be curious. Check out a book. Immerse yourself in something new. So you don't have a wonderful collection of Steuben glass; so you don't jet to foreign capitals. The Prophet Joseph Smith has said, ". . . if a person gains more knowledge and intelligence in this life through his diligence and obedience than another, he will have so much the advantage in the world to come.'' (D&C 130:19.)

Remember: ''The glory of God is intelligence''!

Be Persistent!

Do any of you remember the old Kaiser-Frazer cars? If you do, you obviously are *not* in your teens. But if you don't remember them you really missed something. They were probably ahead of their time. (At least I saw a 1978 model of a well-known make the other day that bears a startling resemblance to one.) Interestingly, however, for whatever reasons, those Kaiser-Frazer cars didn't last. But the man who built them did—Henry J. Kaiser, an amazing man. He made a statement in his later life that bears repeating over and over again. His statement? ''Seventy-five percent of the things I try, fail.'' In light of that statement, consider the other 25 percent:

1. He built 1500 merchant ships during World War II.

2. His mills produced over 1,000,000 tons of steel during the war.

3. During that same time he produced 20,000,000 lb. of magnesium.

4. He became the world's largest producer of cement.

5. He was the third largest producer of aluminum.

6. He helped build the Hoover and Grand Coulee dams.

7. He had a major role in the construction of the San Francisco-Oakland Bridge.

The list goes on and on. Not bad for a 75 percent failure! But he learned one of the keys to life's success: he was absolutely persistent! I repeat, he was *persistent!* Persistence works and pays off to those who possess it.

Not long ago we almost had a tenth member of "The Four Hundred Club." Only nine players in the history of baseball have been able to hit over .400. Do you know the last one? Ted Williams in 1941.

At the beginning of the final week of the season of 1941, Ted's batting average was over .400. His manager asked if he wanted to be excused from playing ball that week so he wouldn't run a chance of losing this average.

"If I'm going to be a .400 hitter," he said, "I'm going to earn the honor fair and square."

Ted's batting average went down a little that last week of the season. Then came the final afternoon of play. Ted's average stood at .39955—not quite .400, but near enough to be counted as such. Sports writers, baseball fans, and even the manager of the team advised him that he should not play that afternoon. They did not want Ted to take a chance on missing the opportunity to become the ninth member of the club.

To them he replied, "If I'm going to be a .400 hitter, I want to have more than my toenails on the line."

The baseball park in Philadelphia was jammed that afternoon. Each time Ted Williams came to bat, the huge crowd sat in tense silence, almost afraid to breathe for fear of upsetting him. Each time he made a hit, the crowd roared its approval. The noise almost rocked Philadelphia when the final game ended and the batting average of Ted Williams stood at .406! How's that for persistence? What a great quality!

Of course, there have been others who persisted. Sir Isaac Newton spent forty years in discovering the law of gravity and gave the credit to his patience. William Cullen Bryant is reported to have written his immortal poem "Thanatopsis" one hundred times before releasing it for publication. Job of the Old Testament stood stripped of his wealth, his children, and the support of his wife and friends, covered with boils and in deep anguish—and refused to give in. His memorable reply was, "Though he [the Lord] slay me, yet will I trust in him." (Job 13:15.) Then, of course, the Savior of this world, hanging on the dreaded cross, after having uttered the words, "My God, my God, why hast thou forsaken me?" (Matthew 27:46), righteously persisted to the end.

Now, those are great examples, but how about John and Mary Doe? How about you and me? Can we have such tenacity? Can we *really* persist like that? The answer is *yes* and the answer rings loud and clear. *We can do it!* Sometimes we can persist because of the love of family members around us; sometimes because of the support of friends who truly care. But there will be other times like those which are portrayed humorously but candidly in a little poem I heard. It's called "Guess Who?"

> "Who comforts me in moments of despair?
> Who runs fingers lightly through my hair?
> Who cooks my meals, darns my hose?
> Squeezes drops into my nose?
> Who always has a word of praise?
> Sets out my rubbers on rainy days?
> Who cheers me up when I'm depressed?
> Makes sure that all my clothes are pressed?
> Encourages me to take a shower?
> And wakes me at the proper hour?
> Who helps to keep me on the beam?
> Who figures in my every dream?
> I do *myself!*"

That's right; sometimes we will have to persist on our own—alone! Those will be the times when no one else can really help. After the prayers and tears, we will have to simply and righteously endure. And we can do it. I *know* we can!

One of my favorite stories of persistence is that of Carrie Jacobs Bond.

"She was left a widow with four thousand dollars in life insurance, a load of debts, and a little boy to support.

"She had had no business experience whatever. She didn't know how to do anything except keep house; and she could hardly do even that, for she had been an invalid for years, her body racked and tortured by the terrible pangs of inflammatory rheumatism.

"But she didn't want pity and she didn't want charity. She was too proud for that. So she cut herself off from all her friends and relatives and went to Chicago to face the grim years ahead.

"She tried running a rooming house, but she couldn't make expenses.

"Then she tried selling hand-painted china that she had decorated herself; but no one wanted her sugar bowls and plates. Next, she tried to write songs; but publishers wouldn't buy them.

"Fifteen years later, Carrie Jacobs Bond was to write 'A Perfect Day,' a song that sold more than six million copies and netted her a quarter of a million dollars in cold cash.

"But when she first started, she couldn't sell her songs for even five dollars apiece. Blighting poverty was her lot. Unable to pay her rent, she often feared that she would be put out on the street. In cold weather, she had to stay in bed to keep warm, for she couldn't burn more than two small bundles of kindling wood each day.

"Finally, she became so poor she could eat only one meal a day; and second-hand dealers took away her furniture and silverware and gave her a little money that kept her from starving.

"But during all this awful poverty and heartache, Carrie Bond continued to write beautiful songs—songs that would one day be sung around the world—songs like 'Just a Wearyin' for You' and 'I Love You Truly.'

"Mrs. Bond wrote these songs on wrapping paper. Because she couldn't afford to buy space in a musical magazine, she sewed dresses for the woman editor in order to pay for the cost of the advertisement.

"At first, she found it difficult to get five dollars an evening for playing and singing her songs; but after she became known, Mrs. Frank J. Mackay, one of the social leaders of England, paid Carrie

Bond one hundred dollars and her expenses to London and back in order to have her sing for only twelve minutes.

"The first time Mrs. Bond tried to sing her songs in vaudeville, she was hissed off the stage. Heartbroken, she fled from the back door of the theater and ran up the street, hatless and coatless, with tears streaming down her cheeks; but years later, her name was featured in electric lights and she was paid a thousand dollars a week for singing in vaudeville.

"She persisted until she overcame all her obstacles, and in so doing, brought happiness to herself and to millions of others." (As told by Dale Carnegie.)

I believe we can do the same. We can righteously persist at whatever we need to do until we accomplish the task. If our task is noble and worthy, we can plead for divine help and receive it; we can receive help from our loved ones; we can obtain encouragement from our friends; and, when necessary, we can persist on our own.

May God enable us to see the vision of things as they can be in our lives if we persist in righteousness.

Look to Others' Needs

2

Marriage in a Throw-away World

Have you seen this year's dress length? Do you know what's the newest trend in sports cars? Have you tried this gadget that makes all others obsolete?

We live today in a plastic world, a throw-away society. It's out with the old and in with the new as we look for shinier, newer, unblemished things.

If yesterday's little girl had broken the leg of her dolly, she would have nursed that toy back to health with love, patience, and a needle and thread and would have loved it all the better for its slight deformity. But if today's child breaks her plastic Barbie, it's into the garbage and back to the store for another—maybe one with a Bermuda tan.

Slick, up-to-the minute, and ultimately replaceable. For better or worse that's life today for most of us. I couldn't help thinking about it at a recent party where Grandma's flowered meat platter that had been passed down three generations sat next to a stack of paper plates.

I've wondered if this restlessness, this endless searching for something more, something shinier, doesn't have something to do with the spiraling divorce rates in our country. It's said that you have a one-in-four chance that the one you court today may be with you in another kind of court tomorrow—divorce court.

Is marriage becoming just another consumer game—if I see a newer model or one with fewer defects, I'll throw the old one out?

The Lord has defined marriage for us. He has said, "For this cause shall a man leave father and mother, and shall cleave to his wife: and they twain shall be one flesh." (Matthew 19:5.)

They twain shall be one. Surely the happiest marriages are those where "your hurt is my hurt; your pain, my pain; your victory, my victory; your vulnerabilities, my own soft spots." But that oneness of heart, of soul, of very flesh, seems to be more of a challenge than ever before in a world where we are conditioned to think, "What's in it for me?" "Are you really meeting my needs?" "Are you making me happy?"

Far too many a marriage partner has become merely an ornament on the arm rather than a part of the heart.

Who killed romance, anyway? One wit said it was killed by the social scientists who renamed everything. People today don't fall in love; they have a "mutual attraction" leading to a "relationship." That doesn't sound nearly as much fun, does it? Couples don't quarrel, kiss, and make up. They have "hostilities," then "clear the air" and "resolve" them.

But I have a different answer to that same question. What killed romance? Selfishness. A terrible overconcern with self. The belief that sacrifice is an obsolete word.

Remember O. Henry's sweet story about a married couple who wanted to give each other the loveliest Christmas gifts they possibly could? She was a sweet young girl, beautiful in every way. But her crown was really the brown cascade of hair that floated over her shoulders. He was a proud, hardworking young man. Still, they were desperately poor.

So as Christmas approached, he looked hard at his proudest possession, the watch that had been his father's and his grandfather's before him. Then he thought of his lovely wife and entered a pawn shop to give up his proud heirloom. With a pawn ticket and a few coins in his hand, he then bought her some tortoise-shell combs with jeweled rims for that lovely head of hair.

When the night came for the gift giving, he gave her the combs he had paid for by giving up his watch. And she, for her part, gave him a platinum watch fob, which she had paid for by selling her beautiful hair.

Their gifts may have seemed useless. But these foolish children in a humble flat were the wisest givers of all. They sacrificed even their dearest possessions for each other.

There's another love story I enjoy. "Soon after he was married, Thomas Moore, the famous nineteenth-century Irish poet, was called away on a business trip. Upon his return he was met at the door, not by his beautiful bride, but by the family doctor.

" 'Your wife is upstairs,' said the doctor. 'But she has asked that you do not come up.' And then Moore learned the terrible truth: his wife had contracted smallpox. The disease had left her once flawless skin pocked and scarred. She had taken one look at her reflection in the mirror and commanded that the shutters be drawn and that her husband never see her again. Moore would not listen. He ran upstairs and threw open the door of his wife's room. It was black as night inside. Not a sound came from the darkness. Groping along the wall, Moore felt for the gas jets.

"A startled cry came from a black corner of the room: 'No! Don't light the lamps.'

"Moore hesitated, swayed by the pleading in the voice.

" 'Go!' she begged. 'Please go! This is the greatest gift I can give you now.'

"Moore did go. He went down to his study, where he sat up most of the night, prayerfully writing—not a poem this time, but a song. He had never written a song before, but now he found it more natural to his mood than simple poetry. He not only wrote the words; he wrote the music, too. And the next morning, as soon as the sun was up, he returned to his wife's room.

"He felt his way to a chair and sat down. 'Are you awake?' he asked.

" 'I am,' came a voice from the far side of the room. 'But you must not ask to see me. You must not press me, Thomas.'

" 'I will sing to you, then,' he answered. And so, for the first time, Thomas Moore sang to his wife the song that still lives today:

" 'Believe me, if all these endearing young charms,
Which I gaze on so fondly today,
Were to change by tomorrow and flee in my arms,
Like fairy gifts fading away,
Thou wouldst still be adored, as this moment thou art—
Let thy loveliness fade as it will,'

"Moore heard a movement from the dark corner where his wife lay in her loneliness, waiting. He continued:

" 'Let thy loveliness fade as it will.
And around the dear ruin each wish of my heart
Would entwine itself verdantly still.'

"The song ended. As his voice trailed off on the last note, Moore heard his bride rise. She crossed the room to the window, reached up and drew open the shutters, then rushed into his arms." (As told by Gaylen Drake.)

Your marriage partner probably doesn't have scars from smallpox, but all of us have defects and imperfections in one way or another. All of us have some irritating habits; all of us have times when our good tempers fail us.

It's not uncommon to hear wives pick at their husbands behind their backs; to hear husbands mourn to other women that their wives just don't understand them; to see wives and husbands fling barbs at each other because of extravagance or sloppiness or insensitivity— defects one can see so clearly in another but can totally fail to see in oneself.

As Richard L. Evans said, "Perhaps any of us could get along with perfect people. But our task is to get along with imperfect people." (*Richard Evans' Quote Book* [Salt Lake City: Publishers Press, 1971], p. 165.)

And William Cowper said it this way:

"The kindest and the happiest pair
Will find occasion to forbear;
Find something, every day they live,
To pity, and perhaps forgive."

Maybe what we need in our marriages is not a new partner but a little more good-natured tolerance. The "psalm of love" in the Bible tells us, "[Love] suffereth long, and is kind." (1 Corinthians 13:4.) And that kind of love, the kind that is not taken lightly nor terminated at pleasure but enables husband and wife to face all of life's little difficulties hand in hand, entwines two souls in the ultimate expression of human happiness.

Fatherhood

Consider the following letter written to a newspaper by a young woman upon the death of her father:

"A great man died today. He wasn't a world leader or a famous doctor or a war hero or a sports figure or a business tycoon. But he was a great man. He was my father.

"He didn't get his picture in the paper for heading up committees. I guess you might say he was a person who never cared for credit or honors. He did corny things—like paying his bills on time, going to church on Sunday, and holding an office in the PTA.

"He helped his kids with their homework and drove his wife to the shopping center to do the grocery buying on Thursday night. He enjoyed hauling his kids and their friends to and from football games. He enjoyed simple things—a picnic in the park, country music, mowing the grass, and running with the dog.

"Tonight is the first night of my life without him. I don't know what to do with myself, so I am writing to you. I am sorry for the times I didn't show him the proper respect. But I am thankful for many things.

"I am thankful because God let me have him for fifteen years.

And I am thankful that I was able to let him know how much I loved him. He died with a smile on his face. He knew he was a success as a husband, a father, a son, a brother, and a friend. I wonder how many millionaires can say that? Thanks for listening; you've been a great help.

"His Daughter"

Isn't that a great tribute! How would you like to receive that kind of eulogy from your child? What kind of world would we have if it had more fathers like that in it? They're certainly needed.

Not long ago a friend of mine was honored by his children. During his birthday celebration all of his children prepared word strips on which they wrote qualities of character which not only described him but had also come to have special meaning to them. His sons and daughters then described personal experiences with their father which exemplified those characteristics. It was a choice time. In sharing that experience, perhaps we can again be reminded that it is not in a single act that a man becomes a great father, but in the continual giving of himself to his children. Ponder the nine qualities of this father as seen through the eyes of his children:

1. *Loving:* "When I'm sick, I can tell he feels bad just because I do. . . . I was lonely and so he bought me a dog. The night the dog was shot, Dad spent the whole night at the animal hospital with me. . . . He always made sure I was in at night before he could go to sleep."

2. *Humorous:* "He's so fun to be around. . . . When things got tense, Dad could somehow make us laugh . . . he's the most clever man I know."

3. *Sensitive:* "He would tenderly offer to give me a blessing if I desired one, not only when I was sick but when I had a big test coming up or when I left for college or had a problem . . . he could sense when I needed help."

4. *Supportive:* "I knew he was busy. Besides, he hates dancing. But he took me to the dance anyway. We had such a great time. . . . He always told me that the greatest investment he could ever make was in his children."

5. *Willing to Help:* "I soon learned that I had to be careful what I asked Dad to do because, no matter how impossible, if he felt

it was a good thing he would try to do it for me. . . . I could *always* count on Dad.''

6. *Trusting:* ''Dad always made me want to do the right thing. I just couldn't disappoint him. . . . When I made a decision, Dad would ask if I had prayed about it and knew that it was the thing to do. If I said yes, he supported me all the way.''

7. *Generous:* ''He and Mom would come to see us with the car loaded with groceries. . . . He is always as free with his time and concern as he is with material things.''

8. *Sentimental:* ''Dad loves family traditions . . . he calls Grandma on her birthday, her wedding anniversary, etc. . . . You always know he'll come up with something special.''

9. *Creative:* ''His presents are really creative. They don't necessarily cost a lot but it's obvious he has taken a lot of time on them. . . . He's sure to have the last word on Christmas morning. He'll have something special up his sleeve. . . . Dad believes every man should find his talents and use them for his children.''

The exciting thing about the experience of my friend is that he's just like you and me. What he has done with his children can be done by every one of us—if we'll just take the time. Time is so important!

Even time for a moment's pause before entering our homes can make a difference. One father reports that each night when he returns home from work, he pauses just before entering the front door and offers a prayer something like this: ''May my presence in this home bring faith and a cheerful good evening to those I love. May my homecoming strengthen my family and bring us closer together, not tear us apart. Keep my voice even, that I may build confidence and respect in me as their father, husband, and friend.''

When I consider all of the qualities we fathers should possess, none is more important than letting our children know we love them. A great prophet once wrote:

''But charity is the pure love of Christ, and it endureth forever; and whoso is found possessed of it at the last day, it shall be well with him.'' (Moroni 7:47.)

Love can overcome a great many problems. Children will be

more patient with our faults if they are sure they are loved. The apostle Peter said it about as well as it can be said:

"And above all things have fervent charity among yourselves: for charity shall cover the multitude of sins." (1 Peter 4:8.)

In other words, we can make parental mistakes of inexperience with our children and they will still respond to us if they know they are loved. And in love, as with all the qualities of a good father, the example we should follow is that of our Eternal Father. There is not a positive quality of fatherhood that we can mention—love, concern, patience, justice, mercy, forgiveness, kindness—that he does not demonstrate continually in our own lives. If we could just remember that our children are his children; our concern for them is his concern; our love for them is his love—at least that's the way it *can* be! We can each become that kind of father. Then, after we have loved and counseled and prayed over a disobedient child who has temporarily gone astray, we will do just as the Father does with us—we won't give up. We'll continue loving. We'll continue trying for as long as it takes. For, after all, we will never be released from our callings as fathers.

I submit that much of our success in this life can and will be measured by the kinds of fathers we are or will become. But it's an eternal circle. I don't believe we will succeed as fathers without first being good husbands. And we won't be good husbands without first being good sons—both to our mortal and Heavenly Parents.

I conclude with a poem by Edgar A. Guest which, I believe, brings perspective to eternal relationships and eternal successes. May we be blessed with this kind of perspective and this kind of success.

A Son—Thoughts of a Father

"We have never seen the Father here, but we have known the Son,
The finest type of manhood since the world was first begun.
And summing up the works of God—I write with reverent pen—
The greatest is the Son He sent to cheer the lives of men.

"Through Him we learned the ways of God, and found the Father's
        love;
The Son it was who won us back to Him who reigns above.
The Lord did not come down Himself to prove to men His worth,
He wrought our worship through the Child He placed upon the
        earth.

"How can I best express my life? Wherein does greatness lie?
How can I long remembrance win, since I am born to die?
Both fame and gold are selfish things; their charms may quickly
        flee;
But I'm the father of a boy, who came to speak for me.

"In him lies all I hope to be, his splendor shall be mine;
I shall have done man's greatest work, if only he is fine.
If some day he shall help the world, long after I am dead,
In all that men shall say of him, my praises shall be said.

"It matters not what I may win of fleeting gold or fame;
My hope of joy depends alone on what my boy shall claim;
My story must be told through him, for him I work and plan;
Man's greatest duty is to be the father of a man."

A Pattern for Good Parenthood

Parents of an energetic and challenging teenager remarked to me the other day, "Do you think we'll make it through the next few years?"

As a father who has reared two teenage daughters and is working with the third, I think I know something of their dilemma. This was illustrated to me several years ago when a colleague of mine asked his teenage daughter to be home from her date by midnight. "But Dad," she protested, "I'm no longer a child." "I know," my friend retorted, "that's why I want you home by twelve." All parents of teenagers are constantly seeking ways to meet the challenge of this age group and close the relationship gap.

There are a number of factors that contribute to healthy home relationships between parents and teenagers. May I suggest to you three which I believe promote the greatest influence for good on your teenage son or daughter?

First: Parents who demonstrate a genuine love and concern for their teenagers.

Children have a way of sensing whether there is a genuine concern for their welfare. You and I know parents who are worried about their own images, the image of the family name, or, in some instances, their own needs. Genuine love for children has some telltale symptoms:

Sincere interest and effort to understand their activities, thoughts, and feelings.

Willingness to listen.

Time spent with them individually.

Being sensitive to their various moods.

These are things that tell a teen you really care.

I know one father who regularly sets time aside each week with his teenagers. (He has three of them.) They call it their time together.

I know a mother who, when her teens come home (there are two), instinctively but caringly greets them with, "Tell me how your day went."

Concern is best demonstrated to teens when they have made mistakes and expect recrimination, but instead get understanding and reassurance.

Second: Parents who practice positive communication with their teenagers.

You will note that I stated this principle as "positive communication." As parents we are always communicating, for good or otherwise. Communication between individuals can be either positive or negative. Too often we communicate negatively without realizing it. Consider the following:

"Are you going to sleep all day? . . . Who said you could use my hairspray? . . . Clean the dishes off the table. . . . Turn down the radio. . . . Have you made your bed? . . . That skirt is much too short. . . . Your closet is a mess. . . . Stand up straight. . . . Somebody has to go to the store. . . . Quit chewing your gum like that. . . . Your hair is too bushy. . . . I don't care if everybody else does have one. . . . Turn down the radio. . . . Have you done your homework? . . . Don't slouch. . . . You didn't make your bed. . . . Quit banging on the piano. . . . Why don't you iron it yourself? . . . Your fingernails are too long. . . . Look it up in the dictionary. . . . Sit up straight. . . . Get off the phone now. . . . Why did you ever buy that record? . . . Take the dog out. . . . You forgot to dust that table. . . . You've been in the bathroom long enough. . . . Turn off the radio and get to sleep now.

"Another day gone, and not once did I say, 'I love you.' "

Too often it is easier to criticize, to point out faults—the negative form of communication which says "I don't like you the way you are"—than to praise or give love. When was the last time you said "I love you" to one of your teenagers? Why not create the opportunity to do it soon?

I know a dad who has made a personal pledge to himself that when practical he will never put off one of his children. He will stop whatever he is doing (his needs) to listen to what his son or daughter wants. Who do you think his teenagers go to when they have problems?

I know another family who try to spend at least an hour at the dinner table. They do this even when one or more of the family members are gone elsewhere. It's a tradition of communication—talking, listening, and laughing together.

May I suggest to you, my fellow parents, that the "gap" in communication between parent and a teen is simply someone who is not listening!

Third: Parents who provide opportunities in the home for spiritual growth.

It's almost a cliché that "today's schools are not doing enough to provide sound, moral education for today's youth." I, for one, agree that the schools can and should do more, but the fact remains that, in the final analysis, this is the parents' greatest opportunity and responsibility.

I believe we should foster close family relationships and give positive inducements to parents to pray with their families, counsel with their children, and sponsor family home evenings every week. We should encourage and show parents how to teach correct principles. The point is that good parenthood is being responsible for the training and development of children. Remember what the Lord has said:

"And again, inasmuch as parents have children in Zion, or in any of her stakes which are organized, that teach them not to understand the doctrine of repentance, faith in Christ the Son of the living God, and of baptism and the gift of the Holy Ghost by the laying on of hands, when eight years old, the sin be upon the heads of the parents.'' (D&C 68:25.)

This can be done in two ways:

1. Have an organized family home evening together once a week, where fundamental principles of integrity, honesty, patriotism, and worship may be emphasized. Such training can be supplemented with fun activities and cultural events.

2. Teach correct principles by parental example.

> "Parents may tell, but never teach,
> Unless they practice what they preach.''
> (Anonymous.)

Here is the tribute of one teenager to her parents: "All the Christianity I really know is what I've seen displayed by my mother and father. Because of them, I feel I know the principles that Christ taught.''

What a tribute!

You remember the lesson behind this little poem:

> "A careful man I want to be,
> A little fellow follows me.
> I do not dare to go astray
> For fear he'll go the selfsame way.
> I must remember as I go
> Through summer's heat and winter's snow—
> I'm building for the years to be
> The little chap who follows me.
> I cannot once escape his eyes;
> Whate'er he sees me do, he tries;
> Like me he says he's going to be,
> This little chap who follows me.''

The lesson still applies with teenagers.

May I share with you an item that came out of the *Chicago Daily News* many years ago? It's titled "A Pattern for Good Parents.''

"A good parent accepts all responsibility for his child—physical, moral, social, and financial. He does not shift his obligation to the school or the church.

"The good parent is unselfish; he does not possess his children completely. When they are adults he expects them to lead lives of their own; when they are younger he trains them to develop independence.

"A good parent remembers that even small children are, above all, human beings with feelings. He never discusses them when they are present or betrays their confidences laughingly to friends and relatives.

"A good parent is consistent in discipline. His child does not get away with murder one day and get trounced for a trifle the next.

"A good parent does not nag his children or complain about them to others. He knows that continual scolding falls on deaf ears.

"A good parent never renders hasty decisions; and once his mind is made up, his child knows that he will be firm. He cannot be coaxed.

"A good parent will be hospitable to his child's friends. His home becomes a pleasant gathering place, and consequently he can subtly guide in choice of associates.

"A good parent will not force his child into or out of any career.

"A good parent is generous with affection. He knows that small children thrive on love expressed, and older children need it, too.''

Making
Memories

Life is a hurried affair for all of us. We rush from task to task, frantic in our chase. Our days sometimes become mere laundry lists of things to do—item 1, item 2, item 3.

And these can seem so all-important, so big to us.

Making a business appointment seems more crucial than telling our sweethearts that we love them; cleaning the house takes first place over reading the little child a story.

On and on we rush until life becomes "full of sound and fury," signifying very little to us.

Have you ever awakened in the morning and realized that not once this week, or this month, or this year, has life really touched you—that not one moment lately has really mattered? Have you ever thought that days and days lie behind you forgotten because they were full, sometimes bursting, with insignificant busyness?

Do you remember the story of a mother who was expecting company for dinner? She had the meat browning in the oven, the cherry pies cooling in the window. So she grabbed a jacket and ran outside where her children were playing. "C'mon, you great kids," she said. "Let's go make a memory."

Together they climbed into the old jeep that was perfect for the canyon, a very short drive away.

They spent an hour collecting rocks in a bag. "Look at this one," said the mother. "Its underside is yellow like a fire."

"Come see this one," she said. "It's been worn by the wind and is smooth."

On the way home from their excursion, bouncing in the jeep, the mother exclaimed in consternation, "Oh no! I forgot to make the rolls for dinner."

"Who cares? Who cares?" said the children. "We're making memories."

And the dinner guests that night didn't even miss the rolls.

What makes a few rare moments in our lives stand out like diamonds in the sand? Why do we cling to certain mental pictures for years when we can hardly remember yesterday morning?

Well, things of the heart last forever! When all of our resounding accomplishments sound empty, when all our glorious material possessions are out-of-date or faded, we remember those magic moments when time stood still and the clouds seemed not to move and we really loved what we loved; when we took the time to show those dearest to us how we felt in the small ways that echo so powerfully in our lives.

Do you remember the apostle Paul's words on love in Corinthians?

"Though I speak with the tongues of men and of angels, and have not [love], I am become as sounding brass, or a tinkling cymbal.

"And though I have the gift of prophecy, and understand all mysteries, and all knowledge; and though I have all faith, so that I could remove mountains, and have not [love], I am nothing.

"And though I bestow all my goods to feed the poor, and though I give my body to be burned, and have not [love], it profiteth me nothing." (1 Corinthians 13:1-3.)

And our lives can seem like so much nothing if we don't take time, conscious time, to make loving memories.

Take the father who often slipped a candy bar under his daughter's books as she studied late for college exams. Take the husband who put a note by his wife's plate at dinner time, thanking her for a fine meal. Take the grandmother who called a little boy to tell him there was a magnificent sunset outside that he really must see.

Little things, really — not expensive, not time-consuming — but oh, what an impact; what memories they make; what love they show.

Here's a story that a young woman, Frances Powler, told about one of those times. It was a day in some ways like any other in her childhood, but she never forgot it.

It was a hectic Saturday in spring, back in the days when the adage "Six days shalt thou labour, and do all thy work" was taken seriously.

Outside, Frances' father and the next-door neighbor, Mr. Patrick, were doing chores.

Inside the houses her mother and Mrs. Patrick were engaged in spring housecleaning. Such a windy March day was ideal for turning out clothes closets. Already woolens flapped on backyard clothes lines.

Frances was hard at work, but somehow her brothers and the Patrick boys had slipped away with their kites to the back lot. Apparently, there was no limit to the heights to which kites would soar that day. Her mother looked out the window. The sky was piercingly blue, the breeze fresh and exciting. Up in all the blueness sailed great, puffy pillows of clouds. It had been a long, hard winter, but today, today was spring.

Then her mother turned to look at the sitting room, its furniture disordered for a vacuum sweeping. The mother hesitated for a minute as her eyes wavered between her work and the window. Finally, she said, "Come on, girls! Let's take string to the boys and watch them fly the kites a minute."

On the way they met Mrs. Patrick and her daughter heading for the back lot and laughing guiltily.

"There never was such a day for flying kites," Frances said. God doesn't make two such days in a century. They played all their fresh twine into the boys' kites, and still they soared. They could hardly distinguish the tiny orange-colored specks. Now and then they slowly reeled one in, finally bringing it dipping and tugging to the earth for the sheer joy of sending it up again. What a thrill for Frances, just a little girl, to run with those kites to the right, to the left, and see their poor, earthbound movements reflected minutes later in the majestic sky dance of the kites. She and the other children wrote wishes on slips of paper and slipped them over the string. Slowly, irresistibly, those wishes climbed up until they reached the kites. Surely, all such wishes would be granted!

Frances remembers that even their fathers dropped hoe and hammer and joined them. Their mothers took their turns, too, laughing like schoolgirls. Her mother's hair, she said, blew out of its pompadour and curled loose about her cheeks; Mother's gingham apron whipped about her lap.

Mingled with the children's fun was something akin to awe. The grown-ups were really playing with them. Frances looked at her mother and thought she actually looked pretty. And she was over forty.

They never knew where the hours went on that hilltop. There were no hours, just a golden, windy day. Parents forgot duty and their dignity; children forgot their competitiveness and small spites. "Perhaps this is the Kingdom of Heaven," Frances thought.

It was growing dark before they all stumbled sleepily back to their houses. There must have been a surface tidying-up, for Frances said the house on Sunday looked decorous enough.

The strange thing was, none of them mentioned that day afterward. Perhaps they were embarrassed that any day could mean so much. Frances locked the memory up in that deepest part of her that we all have—that part where we keep the things that cannot be and yet are.

The years went on; Frances grew up and moved far away from her kite-flying hill. Then one day she was scurrying about her own city apartment, trying to get some work out while her three-year-old daughter insistently cried the desire to "go to the park and see the ducks."

"I can't go," she said. "I have this to do and when I'm through I'll be too tired to walk that far."

Frances's mother, who was visiting, looked up from the peas she was boiling. "It's a wonderful day," she offered. "Really warm, yet there's a fine, fresh breeze. It reminds me of that day we flew the kites.''

Frances stopped in her dash between stove and sink. The locked door flew open and with it a rush of memories. She pulled off her apron. "Come on," she told her little girl. "It's too good a day to miss."

Another decade passed in Frances's life. The world was in the aftermath of a great war. All evening her family had been with one of the Patrick boys, hearing about his experience as a prisoner of war. He had talked freely, but then for a long time had been silent. What was he thinking of—what dark and dreadful things?

"Say," a smile twitched his lips. "Do you remember. . . ? No, of course you wouldn't. It probably didn't make the impression on you that it did on me."

Frances hardly dared speak. "Remember what?" she said.

He answered, "I used to think of that day a lot in prisoner-of-war camps, when things weren't too good. Do you remember the day we flew the kites?"

Winter came, and Frances had the sad duty of paying a condolence call to Mrs. Patrick, recently widowed. She dreaded the call. She couldn't imagine how Mrs. Patrick could face life alone.

At the visit they talked a little of their families and changes in the town. Then Mrs. Patrick was silent, looking down at her lap.

Frances cleared her throat. Now she must say something about the loss, and Mrs. Patrick would surely cry.

But when Mrs. Patrick looked up, she was smiling. "I was just sitting her thinking," she said. "Henry had such fun that day. Frances, do you remember the day we flew the kites?"

A kite-flying day. What was so special about that one day when work was left behind and memories were made? Why did one day sustain so many people through many decades of time?

Make a memory today. Do something to touch the deepest part of you. Consciously decide that you won't let today become one of those yesterdays that was just too full to take the time to love. A single moment may sustain you for years.

Thank God for the memories!

Look to Others' Needs

Keep an
Open Mind

Several years ago my father-in-law, who was at that time a college president, received a letter from a man who desired a position on the college faculty. The letter exuded self-confidence. The applicant claimed to be proficient in fields ranging all the way from foreign languages through music and science to physical education. But in the personal interview which followed, it became clear that the man was not really competent; he was merely conceited. So it often proves to be with the person who thinks he knows everything.

On the other hand, the men and women who have made the truly great, history-changing achievements in this world have usually been sharply aware of their own limitations. They have maintained an open mind toward life and have been ready to learn new things as long as they lived.

Consider Benjamin Franklin, how eagerly he sought new ideas even in his old age. Bacon and Pasteur were constantly seeking new truths. On his deathbed, the great astronomer Laplace said, ''What we know is nothing; what we have to learn is immense.'' Lao-tse, the ancient Chinese teacher, counseled his students with these words: "Be gentle, and you can be bold; be frugal, and you can be liberal. Avoid putting yourself before others, and you can become a leader among men." In popular phraseology another writer has said, "You cannot push yourself ahead by patting yourself on the back."

Isn't that what the Savior taught? "Blessed are the poor in spirit who come unto me." Greek scholars tell us that the word which has been translated "blessed" means almost the same as our English word "happy." Jesus came that we might have life and that we might have it more abundantly. (John 10:10.) He would help each of us to be happy. He would show us how to make the best use of all our God-given talents. He wants us to be successful in our vocations and accomplish every worthy purpose of our lives. To help us do this, he gave as a starting point the first step of the upward climb—*humility.* "Yea, blessed are the poor in spirit who come unto me, for theirs is the kingdom of heaven. . . . And blessed are the meek, for they shall inherit the earth." (3 Nephi 12:3,5.)

These beatitudes are not threats from the Lord; they are statements of basic laws of life. A mind swollen with false pride cannot be easily opened to receive new truth. In a world that changes every day, each hour revealing new truths, the closed mind is destined to mediocrity. As one clever wit has said, "Some people are buried at seventy-five who were dead at thirty." Some teachers, lawyers, doctors, musicians, and men in business and other professions who have the natural ability to achieve great heights in their vocational work nevertheless gradually drift into the background for the simple reason that they cannot see the need for constant growth. They think they have a corner on truth. They have broken the law of humility, and the law of humility is slowly but relentlessly breaking them.

Does this same principle apply to our religious lives? Jesus claimed that it did, and he gave a wonderful example of the operation of the law. "Two men," he said, "went up into the temple to pray; the one a Pharisee, and the other a publican." Let us not forget that they went into the temple *to pray.* If we neglect those two words, we are likely to miss the point of the entire story.

"The Pharisee stood and prayed thus with himself, God, I thank thee, that I am not as other men are, extortioners, unjust, adulterers, or even as this publican.

"I fast twice in the week. I give tithes of all that I possess.

"And the publican, standing afar off, would not lift up so much as his eyes unto heaven, but smote upon his breast, saying, God be merciful to me a sinner.

"I tell you, this man went down to his house justified rather than the other. . . ." (Luke 18:10-14.)

The Pharisee was not an extortioner, nor was he unjust; he did not rob widows, nor did he attempt to crush his weaker competitors. He paid good salaries and gave good measure. At almost every point, he was a better man that the publican. Yet he did not go away justified. His "prayer" had been no more than a boastful listing of his own good qualities and had shown no evidence of a desire for spiritual growth.

The publican, though an unjust tax collector, recognized his weaknesses and opened wide his soul to let the Spirit of God have its way with him. Jesus said, "I tell you, this man went down to his house justified rather than the other: for every one that exalteth himself shall be abased; and he that humbleth himself shall be exalted." (Luke 18:14.)

Jesus did not say that the publican was the better man, nor did he contend that the publican would be more favorably received into the kingdom of heaven. The point Jesus made was that, although both men had come to the temple to pray, only one of them, the publican, had offered a real prayer. The Pharisee could receive no benefit from his prayer because he approached God with a closed mind and with a feeling of self-sufficiency.

Has anyone ever asked you for advice and then spent all of your time attempting to prove to you that his own ideas were right? If so, how did you feel? And how much good would your advice do in such a situation? You cannot help a person who doesn't feel a need to be helped. God could not help the Pharisee, because the self-righteous egotist would not give him a chance.

The only reason God does not help us to develop more likable personalities and more beautiful characters, or to become more successful workers in his kingdom, is that we do not ask with open minds and willing hearts. Most of us have been sufficiently earnest in repeating the first part of the publican's prayer: "Lord, be merciful unto me." But we cannot expect to get good results until we can place an equally sincere and serious emphasis on the rest of the petition: "Lord, be merciful to me—one who needs spiritual growth."

The prophet Jeremiah, when first called to serve God, protested, "Ah, Lord God! behold, I cannot speak: for I am a child. But the Lord said unto [him], Say not, I am a child: for thou shalt go to all that I shall send thee, and whatsoever I command thee thou shalt speak." (Jeremiah 1:6-7.)

Gaining confidence, not from any recognized power of his own but from the promise of the Lord unto him, Jeremiah became a courageous, brilliant statesman and prophet of God, considered by many to be the most forceful and influential in the Old Testament.

Paul, one of the most outstanding apostles of his time, was a brilliant and highly educated man. Yet he spoke of himself as a weak specimen of humanity and chief among the sinners. (Romans 7:19; 1 Timothy 1:15.)

Sir Isaac Newton, discoverer of the law of gravity and one of the greatest scientific thinkers of all time, declared in sweet humility, "I do not know what I may appear to the world, but to myself I seem to have been only a boy playing by the seashore and diverting myself in now and then finding a smoother pebble or a prettier shell than ordinary, while the great ocean of truth lay undiscovered before me."

Abraham Lincoln, tall, sun-crowned man of the ages, frankly admitted to his critics that he may have been the very fool of whom they spoke. When he was criticized for appointing to his cabinet a man who thought himself superior to the president, Lincoln replied that if he knew others of the same caliber he would gladly put all of them in his cabinet.

In light of such noble and successful personalities as these, we should remember, whenever we are tempted to feel haughty or arrogant, that—whether we call it theology, ethics, or just good common sense—the principle of humility is a valid law of life.

Loving and Marriage

The news today is full of marriage, divorce, broken homes, and related challenges. Many radio and television talk shows deal with the subject of love, marriage, and family ties.

Recently I asked a group of married people of varying ages this question: "Do you love your husband (wife)?" Their responses are interesting.

A young girl gave a silly laugh, but no words.

An elderly woman said, "Seems like a foolish question after forty-seven years of marriage, seven children, thirty-four grandchildren, three great-grandchildren, a depression, a world war, and who can remember what else. What do you think?"

A young married woman responded, "I hardly have time to think about that—though I often wonder if he loves me."

An excited young man said, "I'll always love my wife."

A middle-aged man asked, "What difference does it make?"

An old man replied, "The answer to that question is yes, but you young whippersnappers wouldn't have any idea what I'm talking about."

Do you recall the words of the song "Beyond the Promises of Time"? The last verse of that song goes like this:

"Out of the many I will choose just one to share my life,
One that my heart can hold.
Beyond the frail, scant promises of time;
Sealed with a sweetness forever mine."

Beyond the promises of time. Love, true love, cannot be measured by a clock or calendar, for its secret lies in the fullness of eternity. Eternity is a difficult concept for the mortal mind to grasp. Young sweethearts use terms like "forever" and "always" because they seem to sense that the expression of their deepest feelings cannot be captured in the terminology of finite time. Can you imagine yourself marrying a person who tells you that he or she will love you deeply for the next eighteen hours, or for the next three years, or even until death?

There is a new phrase now used by some in their wedding vows, however. They promise to remain together "so long as they love." That very statement has built into it the haunting possibility, if not probability, that their love will end. And there is sufficient evidence now to suggest that it will.

The song spoke of "frail, scant promises of time," echoing the fear of relationships that have built-in termination dates.

As a young man I wondered if I could have a marriage that would endure the passage of time. What would my marriage be after we had lived together for a year, or five years, or twenty? I looked around me and saw many divorces. And even in the marriages that had continued, I saw a great deal of unhappiness, or at best a dull, uninteresting, colorless style of life that reeked of emptiness.

But occasionally I saw a joy that transcended any other form of happiness, and I longed for that to be my way of life. And I suspect I am not so different. Not only do those feelings exist in the young and hopeful, but they continue throughout our lives. Haven't you met some older people who still seemed almost compelled by their feelings of love to reach out and take each other by the hand as though they had been married the day before, even though they had been married forty or fifty years?

Look to Others' Needs

A very touching account comes from a story told by Emma Ray Riggs McKay.

"I accompanied my husband to a dedication of a meetinghouse in Los Angeles. We stopped on Wilshire Boulevard to get our car washed. I sat on a bench and the President was standing over by the car. Suddenly at my elbow I heard a tiny voice say, 'I guess that man over there loves you.' Surprised, I turned and saw a beautiful boy about seven years of age with dark curly hair and large brown eyes. 'What did you say?'

" 'I said, I guess that man over there loves you.'

" 'Why, yes, he loves me; he is my husband. Why do you ask?'

" 'Oh, 'cuz, the way he smiled at you. Do you know, I'd give anything in the world if my Pop would smile at my Mom that way.'

" 'Oh, I'm sorry he doesn't,' I said.

" 'I guess you're not going to get a divorce, then.'

" 'Oh, no, we're not going to get a divorce. We've been married nearly fifty years, and we are very happy. Why do you think that?'

" 'Oh, 'cuz everybody gets a divorce around here. My Pop is going to get a divorce from my Mom. I love my Pop and Mom, and I'—his voice broke and tears welled in his eyes, but he was too much of a little man to let them fall.

"Then he came very close and whispered confidentially in my ear, 'You'd better hurry out of Los Angeles, or you'll get a divorce, too.' And he picked up his papers and shuffled down the sidewalk.

"My heart has bled ever since for that sweet little kiddie, and for all the other youngsters who must suffer because of the nonsensical quarrels of their parents. Mutual tolerance is indeed what we all need." ("The Art of Rearing Children Peacefully." [Provo, Utah: Brigham Young University Press, 1966], p.10.)

What Sister McKay said was true. But there was more to it than that. Those who were well acquainted with David O. and Emma Ray McKay knew that they had lived their lives from the very beginning in a manner that brought them to that wonderful loving relationship even after they had been married almost fifty years. Theirs did indeed become a love that can and will last forever. For them and others like them, eternity is not a meaningless word used only when they were young, for when they were old their love far exceeded that early love and held firmly in its grasp the reality of enduring endlessly.

For those of you who are still very young and are making those choices, keep in mind that out of the many you must choose just one. And that "just one" can be a person that your heart can hold beyond the frail, scant promises of time, sealed with a sweetness that will be forever and ever yours. Don't be a victim of time. Control your impulses. Plan carefully, and you, like David O. McKay, can achieve a loving marital relationship that is full of sparkle, wonder, and joy today and that will endure for all eternity as you step into the tomorrows.

A Cheerful Receiver

Perhaps you remember the old story of the little boy at Christmastime. When his mother told him it was more blessed to give than to receive, he expressed the view that he would like to spread the blessings as widely as possible. It really is more blessed to give than to receive, of course, but one of the best things we can give is a sincere appreciation for the things other people do for us. In the scriptures we are told that "God loveth a cheerful giver." (2 Corinthians 9:7.) And I think we learn in the unwritten Book of Life that the Lord and humanity also love a cheerful *receiver*.

Consider a baby about six months old. Can you imagine a better receiver? He is willing to let us do anything for him: walk him to sleep, feed him, change his diaper, play with him and entertain him by the hour. There is no demand he is reluctant to make, no service he is unwilling to receive. And we love him for it. His trust in our generosity, his unembarrassed acceptance of all we have to give—how much of his appealing charm lies in his willingness to receive.

Almost all babies and very young children are good receivers. But often something happens to us as we begin to grow up, and it becomes harder for us to accept kindness. Perhaps we grow suspicious. We begin to wonder about people's motives. We may say to ourselves when someone offers what appears to be a kindness: "What does he really want? Is he trying to get on my good side so he can get something out of me?" And in our mistrust we may receive the offered kindness coldly and make the giver sorry, so that he is less likely to do a kind deed the next time.

I'm thinking of one such person right now: morally good, anxious to help others, but nearly the most lonesome, woebegone mortal that I know, a man who is actually worrying his life away because he is too blind or too stubborn (and sometimes, I think, too selfish) to acknowledge the kindnesses that others show him. He said recently after some friends had bestowed a kindness upon him, "The only reason they do this is to make me think they're good."

And there are many suspicious souls like him who are missing much of the thrill of life because they are unwilling to take a chance on the natural kindness of human nature. Are they right to be suspicious of people's intentions? I don't think so.

Several years ago I experienced an unexpected illness. During my life I have enjoyed excellent health and have never known many days in bed. Then suddenly this seeming disaster struck. But with it came an unanticipated blessing. During the many weeks and months of recuperation, day in and day out, almost hourly, I found myself showered with human kindnesses from around the world: the little thoughts, the prayers, the flowers, the cards, the letters, the concern of others. This was something I had never experienced before, for I had always been in the kind of work where I was trying to give rather than receive.

What a great blessing I discovered: to be able to accept cheerfully the gracious offers and little helps in my behalf, knowing that they came from the hearts of wonderful Christians and neighbors! Beautiful letters of appreciation, poems, and interesting articles have come from people whose names I have never heard, who have nothing to gain from me, all because they wanted to share their feelings of concern and love and affection. They have extended

Look to Others' Needs

these courtesies because the heart of humanity, when it is not worried or persecuted or in pain, would generally rather be kind than unkind.

The complexities of life today have made us extraordinarily cautious and have so guarded the spirit of kindness that it does not always show on the surface. But if it sees a chance to safely come out in the open, it will be agreeably received. One does not have to look long or far to find himself surrounded on every side by evidences of brotherly appreciation.

It is not only suspicion or distrust of others that can make us bad receivers. Sometimes we find it hard to accept kindnesses because we are too conscientious—or perhaps I should say we are conscientious in the wrong way. Some good people are so anxious to do their part and more, so afraid of placing a burden on others, that it is actually painful to them to receive. You have probably known people like this. There is the woman who cannot receive a plateful of cookies without paying you back with a full-course meal. Or there is the man who cannot accept a few minutes' help in getting his stalled car going again without feeling he has taken on an immense obligation.

When the Savior told the parable of the Good Samaritan, he was mainly concerned with making the point that we should give freely to those who are in need of help. Therefore, he didn't say how the man who had been robbed and beaten responded to the Good Samaritan who gave him aid. But can we imagine that the Good Samaritan would have been pleased if the man had gone to great lengths to seek him out and repay the debt with interest? I think not. The kind act was done freely and, I hope, received as freely.

We should not think of kindness as a credit-card system in which we incur burdensome debts when we accept something—or in which others become our debtors when we do something for them. Instead, we might appropriately think that whenever we either give or receive kindness we are adding to the total wealth of happiness in the world. If we receive gladly, we can gladden the heart of the giver, who will feel abundantly repaid for his efforts when he sees that they have been received in the spirit he intended. And when we learn the skill to receive gladly, we are ready to give just as gladly when the opportunity arises—not out of a sense of obligation or to repay a debt, but out of a spirit of love, happy to live in a world where people do things for one another.

It is indeed true that "God loveth a cheerful giver," and one of the best things to give is a cheerful acceptance of what others give to you.

The Worth of a Child

A neighbor told my mother some time ago, "I see that your son has produced another book."

Mother, recalling the days of my youth when I had problems in school, said, "Yes, but I doubt if he can read it."

Mother may have had her doubts about me, as mothers sometimes do, but I'm glad she didn't give up.

Have you heard that commercial that says: "Give your children everything; give them your time"? I wonder how many of us wince with guilt when we hear that little phrase. "Give your children everything; give them your time." It's not that we wouldn't like to give our children our time, but sometimes life makes us impatient or tired or bored or too busy for the kids. In our running and chasing for what we want out of life, we forget the infinite worth of what we already have in our own homes.

When a child scatters toys through every room and spills milk on the newly waxed floor, in our anger we see only the worth of a clean house.

When a teenager turns up rock music until our heads are pounding, we think of the worth of an hour of silence.

When a son brings a story to be read just as our favorite TV show comes on, we think of the worth of "Sixty Minutes" or "Kojak" or "Gunsmoke."

Business appointments. A new car. The job at hand. These things have worth to us. But who can even begin to calculate the worth of a human soul?

Could you attach a price tag to a soul? When I was back in Boston a few years ago, a man was walking along a bridge overlooking Boston Harbor. It was a cold day but with something of an early spring in the air. He happened to look over the bridge and saw a little dog out on a cake of ice in the harbor. He made a telephone call to the Boston Police Department. Policemen rallied to the call, but surmised quite early that they did not have the facility to retrieve this dog, so they called the Boston Fire Department. As things will often happen in communication, some eight ladder companies answered the call. You ought to see a ladder truck trying to get down a Boston street. Well, when they got there, they couldn't quite figure out how to get this dog, literally floating out to sea, off the cake of ice. So they called for some additional emergency equipment. One enterprising reporter, sizing up the situation, did some fast calculations and surmised that in about a six-hour effort the city of Boston had paid several thousands of the taxpayers' money to get one mongrel dog out of the harbor. I'm not here to debate the value of a dog. My daughter would tell you that it was worth it. We have one.

But what would you spend to save a child? Would any amount of money be too much? Listen to this newspaper account.

At 4:45 on a Friday afternoon in April 1949, a laughing three-year-old child was playing with her small friends in a grassy vacant lot beside her home. Suddenly she disappeared. She had fallen into a long-abandoned well. Fifteen minutes later her mother called the police and reported that her daughter was wedged in a rusty old shaft. Half an hour later firemen were pumping oxygen into the small opening. At the end of an hour, efforts to raise Kathy with a rope had failed, and at 6:00, power equipment began digging a parallel hole. During this brief time the girl called back bravely to the familiar world above her. She always answered those she loved with courage: "Yes, I'm all right." She wanted to please. "Will you try to grab hold of the rope, Kathy?"

"I am. I am." Then her voice ceased, but she had spoken long enough to convince those above her that she was unhurt by her fall.

"By the time I reached the lot, it was no longer vacant," said the reporter. "Under a blaze of light, men and machines began to battle with Mother Earth. Men by the hundreds began to volunteer their help. Circus midgets living in the vicinity arrived and risked being lowered by their feet into the crumbling old shaft. There were Boy Scouts, long thin men, acrobats, engineers, firemen and waving hands. All were drawn by the human drama, wanting to help. By daybreak people throughout the world were invisible spectators. Newspapers, radio, and television put aside war and international news to headline the story of a desperate rescue attempt."

Bill Yancy, a thirty-eight-year-old contractor, moved back five feet of earth in less than half an hour.

A boilermaker stayed at his dangerous job beneath the ground until he collapsed with the stabbing pain of a hernia and was rushed to the hospital—all this to save a three-year-old.

But that's not all.

The father of five children sneaked out of his own home to volunteer his help although he had not done any deep excavation work for a long time. "I didn't want to worry my wife," he said, "but I have five good reasons at home."

The hole parallel to the well reached the fifty-seven-foot level early Saturday morning. That night workers hit a sand pocket, and water flowed into the tunnel. Pumping began desperately. Seldom had so much prayer power been focused on one person or on any one rescue.

Men on a lonely watch on a ship far at sea followed the progress and took up a collection. Coal miners in Denver had offered help. A neighbor brought a chocolate cake. One unidentified man brought over seven hundred gallons of coffee and stacks of doughnuts to serve the workers.

Meanwhile, sitting side by side in a parked car during most of these frantic operations were the girl's white-faced mother and father. Beneath the giant machines, bright lights, and rigging lay a tiny figure. Was all well with her? Was there water where she lay? Did she know moments of consciousness and fear?

Fifty-three hours from the time this episode began, after a total expenditure of half a million dollars, Bill Yancy was lowered into the rescue shaft on a bucket fastened to the end of a cable. Then the answer came up. Kathy Fiscus, the little girl whom the whole world had come to know, was dead. She had gone shortly after she had last spoken.

Was that effort worth it? Half a million dollars and countless man hours went into that rescue attempt. Is one child really worth all that trouble?

I recall an incident in the life of Horace Mann, the great educator. He was speaking at a dedicatory service for a new school. In the course of his remarks he said, "The great investment we have made together for this building will be worth it all, if we save but one child."

Following his address he was approached by one who challenged him: "Didn't you overstate that just a trifle?"

"Not if that one child were mine," he replied.

Somehow, it's easy for us to see the worth of a child when we are talking about life-and-death events or moments of high drama. We all agree that we would give any amount of time to save a helpless child in a well shaft; we would spend any amount of money to spare our own child from misery or harm. But in those countless undistinguished moments we do spend with our children, we seem to forget their ultimate worth.

"John, if you had come home at a decent hour last night, you wouldn't be so tired this morning." "Jenny, you still haven't cleaned up that mess in your room. I can't count on you for anything." "Who left the lights on in the basement?" "Whose turn was it to take out the garbage?" Those are the kinds of things we say to our children, and with every comment we chip away at their feelings of worth. We treat them with less appreciation, less sensitivity, less old-fashioned courtesy than we would a stranger on the street.

The worth of a child; the incalculable worth of a human soul. Do we really think of that when we tell our children, "Not now; I'm too busy,'' or ''Don't bother me with that''? In the balance, rearing your children is the most important thing you do. The buildings you build will crumble with age; governments will come and go; today's best-seller will yellow with time. But a child, a human soul, is eternal. The time you give in loving and shaping a human personality is an investment in the eternities.

Give your children everything; give them your time. John Gunther, a father who wrote a book about his son's early death of brain cancer, says this: ''While you still have sons and daughters, embrace them with a little added rapture and a keener awareness of joy.'' May we all be so inclined.

Look
Around You

3

Faces

Faces! Smiling, frowning, angry, calm, unhappy, content. Faces! Round, square, oval, dimpled, beautiful, plain, striking, ordinary. Faces! Old and young.

I must admit I am a "people watcher." There's not anything much more interesting than watching people.

Is there anything quite so revealing as the face of a boy at his birthday party; of a young couple just engaged; of new parents with their first child; of a proud mom and dad at their child's graduation; of a husband and wife on their golden wedding anniversary?

Is there anything quite so funny as the face of a six-year-old with bubble gum exploded from ear to ear; of a "forgetful" girl with two dates for the same night; of a young bride who innocently cooks the peas in the pod; of a parent who calls every name in the house before finding the right one; of Grandpa without his teeth in?

And finally, is there anything quite so touching as the face of a child in prayer; of a teenager alone in a new school; of a young couple upon the death of their first child; of parents worried sick over a wayward child; of old people unvisited and unloved?

Faces! They reveal so much! They tell a story. There's a great little poem I know about faces that says so well what needs to be said:

It Shows in Your Face

"You don't have to tell how you live each day;
You don't have to say if you work or you play;
A tried, true barometer serves in the place—
However you live, it will show in your face.

"The false, the deceit that you bear in your heart,
Will not stay inside where it first got a start;
For sinew and blood are a thin veil of lace—
What you wear in your heart, you wear in your face.

"If your life is selfless, if for others you live,
For not what you get, but how much you can give;
If you live close to God in his infinite grace—
You don't have to tell it, it shows in your face."

I don't know of anything more true than that. As was once said of President David O. McKay: "He carries his letter of recommendation in his countenance." Faces somehow tell it all.

Do you remember the story of "The Great Stone Face" by Nathaniel Hawthorne? You'll recall that the great stone face was a work of nature; it was a mountain so constructed that, from a distance, it had the appearance of a face—a divine, majestic face. You'll also recall that the hero of this great story was Ernest, a man who waited all his life to see the prophecy concerning the great stone face fulfilled: that someday a man would come to the valley who would be so good, so kind, so honorable that he would look exactly like the mountain—the great stone face. But Ernest waited in vain. For although several men came to the valley who purportedly had these qualities which made them appear to be "the great stone face," none actually did.

A wonderful thing takes place by the end of the story. Ernest himself takes on the image of the great stone face. Slowly but surely over the years, from a young boy to an old man, Ernest himself becomes the fulfillment of the prophecy.

As I reread the story the other day, I noted some of the adjectives Hawthorne used to describe Ernest during the story: dutiful, helpful, mild, loving, tender, industrious, kind, neighborly, and so on. Toward the end of the story he gave the key that explained why Ernest's own face had become that of the great stone face. Let me quote:

"His words had power, because they accorded with his thoughts; and his thoughts had reality and depth, because they harmonized with the life which he had always lived. . . . Not a day passed by that the world was not the better because this man, humble as he was, had lived."

What a compliment! Not one day passed but that the world was made better because of him. No wonder Ernest's face looked special. He *was* special!

There are people like Ernest all around us. And there are many of us trying to *become* like him. And, just as surely as night follows day, the more we try, the more such effort is mirrored in our faces.

There is another story told of George Hall. It is a fictitious story, but a significant one.

"Lord George had led an evil life. He had been a drunkard, a gambler, and a cheat in business, and his face reflected the life he had led. It was a very evil face.

"One day he fell in love with a simple country girl to whom he proposed marriage. Jenny Mere told him that she could never marry a man whose face was so repulsive and so evil looking, and also that, when she did marry, she wanted a man with a saint-like face which was the mirror of true love.

"Following a custom of the day, Lord George went down to Mr. Aeneas in Bond Street, London. Aeneas made waxen masks for people, and his skill was so perfect that the person's identity was completely hidden. As proof of his skill, it was said that many spendthrift debtors, equipped with his masks, could pass among their creditors unrecognized. Aeneas went to his storeroom, selected a mask, heated it over a lamp, and fixed it to Lord George's face; and when Lord George looked in the glass, he had the face of a saint who loved dearly. So altered was his appearance that Jenny Mere was soon wooed and won.

"He bought a little cottage in the country, almost hidden in an arbor of roses, with a tiny garden spot. From then on his entire life changed. He became interested in nature; he found 'sermons in stones, books in brooks, and good in everything.' Formerly he was blasé, and life had no interest for him; now, he was engrossed in kindliness and the world around him.

"He was not content with starting life anew, but tried to make amends for the past. Through a confidential solicitor he restored his ill-gotten gains to those whom he had cheated. Each day brought new refinements to his character, more beautiful thoughts to his soul.

"By accident, his former companions discovered his identity. They visited him in his garden and urged him to return to his old evil life. When he refused, he was attacked, and the mask was torn from his face.

"He hung his head. Here was the end of all; here was the end of his newfound life and his love dream. As he stood with bowed head, with the mask at his feet on the grass, his wife rushed across the garden and threw herself on her knees in front of him. When she looked up at him, what do you suppose she found? Lo! Line for line, feature for feature, the face was the same as that of the mask."

What a wonderful story! We *do* take on the appearance of our thoughts, our desires, our actions. Remember what Solomon said: "As [a man] thinketh in his heart, so is he." (Proverbs 23:7.)

Children often look like their parents. But despite physical inheritances, there is something more important that determines beauty. Clean thoughts, kindly actions, a pleasant disposition—those are the *real* determiners of outward appearance.

The prophet Alma once asked his people a very penetrating question, which I now ask you:

"And now behold, I ask of you, my brethren of the church, have ye spiritually been born of God? Have ye received his image in your countenances? Have ye experienced this mighty change in your hearts? . . .

"I say unto you, can ye look up to God at that day with a pure heart and clean hands? I say unto you, can you look up, having the image of God engraven upon your countenances?'' (Alma 5:14, 19.)

I believe that's a fair question we all should ask ourselves. Are we, through our thoughts and actions, reflecting the influence of the Lord upon us? Is there any difference between you and someone who has no faith? Or, if you are one without faith, are you striving to get it? It will make a difference in the way you look. It will make an eternal difference.

May we be honest enough to answer these questions truthfully. And may we have the courage to make necessary changes where required.

Living the gospel makes a difference even in the way we look. We mirror what we are, and we *all* can be beautiful children of a loving Heavenly Father by thinking and acting as he would have us do. It is a lifelong pursuit, but eternally worth the effort.

The Quiet Heroes

Have you ever noticed how some people seem to get all the glory? Pick up a magazine and there they are in glossy color—the superstars, the sports heroes, the executive tycoons. We hang on what they wear, what they do, and what they think. They seem to go to glamorous places and live days that are larger than life.

We see the flashy ones around us, too, who bask in the community limelight and enjoy the adulation of others.

And through all this hoopla I cannot help but ask, do we really know who the heroes are? Is heroism really so loud, so flashy, so aware of itself?

As Thomas Carlyle said, ''When the oak is felled, the whole forest echoes with its fall, but a hundred acorns are sown in silence by an unnoticed breeze.''

Sometimes it's the unassuming ones, those who work quietly at some noble task, who are life's real heroes.

I had an experience that every man, and I suppose every boy, has had at one time or another in his life. I was dressing to go to work and had just about completed the task when I discovered that my last clean white shirt was missing the collar button.

Everything else was ready—shoes shined, clothes pressed, hair combed—even my necktie was selected. But by its absence, one tiny, missing button slowed up the whole progress of the day.

Well, the button was sewn back in place, and all was right again. But I learned something very profound. With all those flashy neckties to choose from, my well-being was completely dependent upon one little collar button.

The world is similarly disturbed, and greatly hindered in its work, because there are too many human neckties—too many people who want to show off in the front of the crowd—and too few who want to work in the background at some task of equal or greater importance where the personal credit is small.

Take the seemingly commonplace man, middle-aged, a little bald, who always seemed tired, and was slow to speak. You wouldn't pick him out for a hero by any chance.

But this man was eloquent in another way, a way that very few of his own friends knew. His wife, an invalid of fifteen years, needed constant care. They could never afford a round-the-clock nurse. So night after night, year after year, he sat up by her bed keeping a vigilant watch. His only sleep for all those years consisted of catnaps caught in his chair as he watched over the sickbed of his sweet wife.

Who are the heroes? The superstars?

Take the humble woman who gathered old clothes from neighbors and friends and strangers. Twenty years she did this, keeping her sewing machine busy putting the discards back into perfect shape—a button here, a seam there. And when each new load was cleaned and pressed and perfect, she took it to the state training school where hundreds of mentally handicapped children rejoiced in their "new" clothes.

Who are the heroes? The superstars?

Here is a poem by Carol Lynn Pearson that asks the same question.

The Cast

"I lost the starring part in Our Town
To Linda, a girl not half as good as me,
Who kept her eyes down
For the whole tryout, and even stuttered.

"When the cast was posted
And the high school drama coach
Saw me reading it through my tears,
He put an arm around me and said,
'Now, look—things are not always as they appear.
This is not Broadway;
It's an educational institution.
We're here for two reasons—to put on a show,
And, more important, to help people grow.
Someday you'll see.'

"So Linda played Emily,
And she didn't even stutter,
And I was Third Woman at the Wedding,
Watching and wondering how he knew
What she could really do
If she had the chance.

"Since then I have guessed that God
Being a whole lot smarter
Than my high school drama coach,
Might be offstage sometimes
With an arm around a questioning cast:
'Now, don't try to outguess me.
Sometimes the first shall be last
And the last shall be first,
And I've got my own reasons.
I need some strong ones to star
And some strong ones to stand back.
And I'm going to put out front

Some you might not choose,
But you'll see what they can really do
When they have the chance.
Mortality is an educational institution,
We've got to put on the show,
And, too, we've got to help people to grow.'

"As I walk through the scenes,
Watch the costumes move,
And listen to the lines
Of the powerful, the weak,
The rich, the poor,
I look at the leads with less awe than most,
And at the spear-carriers with more."

> (From *The Growing Season* by Carol Lynn Pearson,
> published by Bookcraft. Copyright © 1976 by
> Bookcraft, Inc. Used with permission.)

Who are the heroes? The superstars?

It was the greatest of us all, whose brilliance in intellect, beauty, and compassion is infinite, even the Lord and Master, Jesus Christ himself, who said, "And whosoever will be chief among you, let him be your servant: Even as the Son of man came not to be ministered unto, but to minister. . . ." (Matthew 20:27-28.)

And it was Jesus, at the Last Supper, who took a towel and basin and performed that completely humble act: he washed the disciples' feet—feet that were dusty and hot from walking sandaled in the streets of Jerusalem; feet that were creased with dirt from many long miles of following him.

Who are the heroes? The superstars?

Surely the ultimate lesson in heroism was given us by Christ himself, whose life teaches us that we cannot tell who is great by the applause of the crowd, by the honors afforded in slick magazines or popularity contests.

The heroes are all of us who, without pomp or ceremony, perform our daily tasks with care—no matter who is looking. The heroes are those who love well, work hard, and serve selflessly without the need for glory.

And though we make a big thing of some people, give them a bigger slice of the pie, a softer seat, the truth is this: "We are all little men when the stars come out."

God bless us to remember this.

America—
Thank Heaven

Consider the following description of a truly remarkable person:

"He hears an airplane overhead, and if he looks up at all, he does so in security, neither in fear nor in the hope of seeing a protector.

"His wife goes marketing, and her purchases are limited by her needs, tastes, and budget, but not by decree.

"He comes home on an evening through streets which are well lighted, not dimly in blue.

"He reads his newspaper, and knows that what it says is not concocted by a bureau, but is an honest, untrammeled effort to present the truth.

"He adheres to a political party to the extent that he desires and reserves the right to criticize any of its policies—even if his convictions dictate that the theory of government of the country is wrong and should be scrapped.

"He does not believe, if his party is out of power, that the only way in which it can come into power is through a bloody revolution.

"He converses with friends, even with chance acquaintances, expressing freely his opinion on any subject, without fear.

"He does not expect his mail to be opened between posting and receipt, nor his telephone to be tapped.

"He changes his place of dwelling, and does not report so doing to the police.

"He has not registered with the police.

"He carries an identification card only in case he should be the victim of a traffic accident.

"He thinks of his neighbors across international borders as though they were across a state line, rather than as foreigners.

"He worships God in the fashion of his choice, without fear.

"He should struggle to preserve his Americanism with all its priceless privileges.

"He is a fortunate man—*He is an American.*"

(Editorial, *New York Sun.*)

Each one of you is also a very fortunate person. I, too, am a blessed man, and I thank heaven. Thank heaven for America! Despite our weaknesses, despite our problems, despite our challenges, this is the greatest nation on earth. As someone once said, "We haven't done badly for a nation of immigrants!"

But we haven't done it alone. We have done it because God helped us to do it. Our gratitude for America should be to him. I think you'll remember with me George Washington's statement at the conclusion of the convention at which the Constitution was adopted. These are his words:

"We have raised a standard to which the good and wise can repair; the event is in the hands of God. . . .

"Now, therefore, I do recommend and assign Thursday the 26th of November next to be devoted by the people of these States to the service of that great and glorious Being, who is the beneficent Author of all the good that was, that is, or that will be, that we may then all unite in rendering unto Him our sincere and humble thanks. . . ."

That proclamation might very well be given each of the 365 days of the year. Ought we not to be grateful for this great land?

I thank heaven for the freedom in this country to enjoy the

myriad of small, seemingly insignificant things that we so often take for granted. Just for a moment, look with me through the eyes of a marvelous Russian immigrant, Nila Magidoff. She married her husband, Robert, an American correspondent in Moscow, and later was forced to leave Russia. Let me share just a paragraph from her story:

"One day, I took my first ride in the New York subway. I missed all my connections, not because of the movement of the trains, but because of the movement of the many faces. It was then that I remembered the first time in my life I saw chewing gum. It was not in this New York subway. It was in the Moscow subway. Two beautiful American girls, tourists, were talking and chewing gum. Not one Russian moved from that train. When the Americans left, all the Russians left. Sitting next to me was an elderly Russian man. He looked at the girls and said, 'What a pity. Such beautiful girls and such a strange nervous disease.' "

Imagine any of us being thankful for gum! But there's a spirit in that little experience I hope you can feel.

Now, one more glance through Nila's eyes while she still lived in Russia:

"While I was waiting for permission to come to America, Robert went alone three times. I will never forget the excitement when he used to come back and bring with him all kinds of American gadgets. You see, you Americans don't know how much they meant, these little things, to the Russian people, because there was always a shortage of consumer goods and because of our naive and childish curiosity for all kinds of gadgets.

"I remember once Robert brought an electric toaster. It was a toaster that every one of you owns, that every one of you uses every day, but no one ever notices. Not me! When I got a toaster, I telephoned all my Russian friends, 'Please come for American toast.' We put the toaster in the middle of the table. We put in two pieces of bread and waited without even breathing. You know, the bread 'jumped out,' and then we put butter on it. Eight of us—we ate ten pounds of American toast!"

Chewing gum, toast, sugar cubes, popcorn, *Sports Illustrated,* hair dryers, Pampers, washing machines, TV, cars, homes, families! We have so much. Thank heaven for America!

The spirit of gratitude for this great land that I wish we all could feel is found in an experience I once had. While I was serving in the infantry during World War II, it was my privilege as an American soldier to be engaged in a number of battles. During one of those campaigns on an island in the Pacific, my particular platoon drew the assignment to secure a military objective several miles into the jungle. On our reconnaissance, lo and behold, we came upon an enemy concentration camp. Incarcerated in this camp were some 2,500 to 3,000 natives. The enemy had abandoned the camp several minutes before, and I was honored to be one of the few soldiers to break down the barriers and bring freedom to this anxious group.

Words cannot describe the filth and misery that these people had experienced during their three years of imprisonment. Many children had been born under this extreme condition, where sickness and malnutrition were rampant. As we were hastily preparing to evacuate these unfortunate people to the beach area, I was standing inside the camp and was startled to feel a thump on my boot. Looking down in the mud, I found the form of a man, perhaps in his sixties, who was barely recognizable as being alive. Upon examining him closer, I found that he was an American minister who had been trapped in the jungle and eventually taken prisoner by the enemy. Even though he was approximately six feet tall, he weighed less than a hundred pounds, and huge sores covered his body.

As he struggled to gain some strength, his first request of me was, "Soldier, do you have an American flag?" I told him I did not have one with me, but I thought I could secure one. After sending word to one of our jeep drivers to see if he could find one, we prepared a stretcher and tried to bring the man as much physical comfort as possible under those conditions. We cleaned the mud from his face, gave him a drink of water, and administered minor first aid. When the flag was brought to us, I handed it to him. With tears in his eyes, he placed it over his bosom and said, "Thank God you have come!" And I, an eighteen-year-old soldier, saw in the face of a man who had experienced terrible tragedy the true meaning of freedom and of America. Thank heaven for America!

Now, my friends, may we not be ungrateful. In referring to the physical and spiritual blessings we enjoy, including those in this land, the Lord has given us this counsel, which is scripture: "And in nothing doth man offend God, or against none is his wrath kindled, save those who confess not his hand in all things, and obey not his commandments." (D&C 59:21.)

We need to look around us and be thankful. As bad as our situation in this country sometimes looks, there is great hope if we give thanks to him who is the giver of all our blessings. That gratitude, together with a determination to keep his commandments and live good and honest lives, will see us through. I conclude with the words of a well-known hymn of praise:

> "Our fathers' God to thee,
> Author of liberty,
> To thee we sing.
> Long may our land be bright
> With freedom's holy light.
> Protect us by thy might,
> Great God, our King!"
> (Samuel F. Smith, "My Country, 'Tis of Thee.")

May our righteousness as individuals and as a nation be such that that prayer will be answered upon this great land.

Learn to
Love the Storm

Years ago, a columnist for a Wisconsin newspaper wrote this tribute to his mother the day she died: "She taught me to love the storm." He described how, as a child, he had been terrified of thunder and lightning. When the big, dark clouds came rolling in and the sound of lightning cracked outside his window, he used to hide, trembling, in his closet. But his mother always came for him during these storms and, taking him by the hands, led him to the front porch, where the heavenly violence could be seen in all its force. There she described the grandeur of a nature that could produce these things, the beauty of the jagged flashes of light across the sky. And gradually the boy "learned to love the storms. And all the things that make storms in life— controversy, reverses, criticism—no longer terrified me."

My own mother, who had been so taught by her father, did a similar thing with her children.

Storms are an inevitable part of weather. We simply couldn't exist on earth without the wind or the gray, damp days that bring us rain.

And storms are inevitable in each of our lives. Adversity is to life what stormy weather is to nature. Most of us have experienced some disappointment or heartache. A loved one dies, we face ill health, we miss an opportunity, we have a nagging worry, we think nobody cares about us—all these things can make us feel as if the thunder clouds are gathering around us with crushing force.

How do we learn to live with our stormy days?

Some people let reverses embitter them. They decide the world is a terrible place to be, and "die" long before they're buried.

A widow who had faced some setbacks in life just pulled her shades against the world. She became the neighborhood grouch, even going so far as to fill with water any cars that were accidentally parked in front of her house.

As one wit said, "You never know what makes some people tick until they begin to unwind."

But others handle their disappointments in life with far better grace. Take, for instance, the man who'd been seriously ill with scarlet fever as a child and almost completely deaf from the beginning of his adolescence. At age six he accidentally set fire to his father's barn, for which he was whipped in public as an example to the other children.

His family was so poor he couldn't go to school, so he was set to work at an early age. He was discharged from many of his jobs because he didn't fit in. And there were times when, for lack of money, he subsisted for days on end on only one meal.

Who was this man who apparently faced more than his share of life's stormy days? Thomas Edison—the same man who said he had discovered a thousand things that didn't work before he found the right material for the filament of the light globe.

The darkest day for Scottish essayist and historian Thomas Carlyle was when his friend John Stuart Mill came to visit and said: "I don't know how to tell you this—but you remember the manuscript you gave me to read? Well, the maid used it to light the fire."

Carlyle was first enraged, then grieved. At last a deep melancholy settled over him that he could hardly shake. Then one day he sat by his window and saw bricklayers at work. "It came to me," he said, "that as they laid brick on brick, so could I lay word on word, sentence on sentence."

With that he began to rewrite *The French Revolution,* a classic that endures to this day as a monument to one man's ability to handle his private storms.

Still, when most of us face heartache, our first thought is to cry to the Lord to be saved from it all. We want him to lift it all away. How familiar are these prayers: "Dear Lord, don't let this happen to me;" or, "Let this not be true;" or, "Please, please, anything but this!"

And it is one of life's most sobering lessons that our Father in heaven, loving as he is, doesn't always remove our heartaches from us. We may pray fervently for sunshine, and the storm still may come. And in the seeming rejection of our prayerful petitions, we may retreat to disillusionment. "How can there be a God?" we may ask. "If there is, how can he allow me to be in such pain?"

The Prophet Joseph Smith, when experiencing a period of great difficulty and adversity, prayed:

"O God, where art thou? And where is the pavilion that covereth thy hiding place? How long shall thy hand be stayed, and thine eye, yea thy pure eye, behold from the eternal heavens the wrongs of thy people and of thy servants, and thine ear be penetrated with their cries? . . . Let thy hiding place no longer be covered; let thine ear be inclined; let thine heart be softened. . . . Remember thy suffering saints, O our God; and thy servants will rejoice in thy name forever." (D&C 121:1,4,6.)

And the Lord responded:

"My son, peace be unto thy soul; thine adversity and thine afflictions shall be but a small moment. . . . The Son of Man hath descended below them all. Art thou greater than he?" (D&C 121:7; 122:8.)

Adversity, then, is a part of the eternal plan. We gain strength and power by overcoming.

A stately tree grew by a church in one city where it was nurtured by warm sun and gentle rains. And then one day a rough wind blew it over, revealing shallow roots. The tree had had it too good. It didn't have to send down sturdy, steadying roots in search of food or water. Unlike the old mountain cedar, born to wind and sleet, this tree had no need for a tough center and clinging roots.

God's love for us is made of stern stuff. He cannot give us everything we ask for, he cannot help us sidestep all suffering, for the result would be fragile souls with shallow roots. He doesn't want us to be whiners, complainers, or tremblers in the closet. We are God's children, and, like any loving parent, he cannot be satisfied with us until we have a certain character, a certain nobility. He wants us to become like him.

Then what can we expect from the Lord when we pray for help in times of crisis? The greatest bounty of all. Sparrows crossing a superhighway by hopping may not realize they have the power to rise above the danger coming at them from all sides, but we can. God can give us power to face life on lifted wings. He can give us the strength, the silent courage, to—like Edison—overcome sickness or humiliation and invent a light bulb. He can give us the steady perseverance so that—like Carlyle—we can, day by day, overcome the deepest melancholy.

As the English pastor Canon Westcott said: "Great occasions do not make heroes or cowards; they simply unveil them to the eyes of men. Silent and imperceptibly, as we wake or sleep, we grow strong or weak; and, at last, some crisis shows us for what we have become."

Learning to love the storm may be the greatest secret for triumphant living—to move from the closets where we hide to the front porch where we can see the glory of the sky and feel the strength of the Lord. For it may be as we nobly endure our darkest days that we overcome our terror of the storm.

The Wonder
of It All

The other day I was reading an old issue of the *Reader's Digest*. I found great interest in a number of statements quoted in an article entitled "No Wonder."

For example, an old rancher who looked down into one of nature's great marvels, Utah's Bryce Canyon, said, "It'd be a bad place to lose a cow in."

And then there was the charwoman who visited Carisbrooke Castle on the Isle of Wight. In its small museum were several suits of armor. Looking at them, the crowd was enthralled with the long avenues of the past they represented. The charwoman took one glance at the armor and said with disgust to her friend, "Oh, I wouldn't like to have to clean that every week."

What does a rancher in one part of the world have in common with a charwoman in another? Unfortunately, something we all share on occasion. It's a kind of blindness. Oh, it wouldn't be measurable on an optometrist's chart, but it's a sight problem all the same. We see the world with a film over our eyes. We've lost the awe of wonder.

The article goes on to say, "There are people all over the world eating their hearts out to travel and see wonders which are far away. Yet most of them are blind to wonders near at hand. In familiar events of the familiar world about me, which I dismiss as utterly trifling, Shakespeare would find the material for a play."

Here, for example, is how one man saw an apple—a plain, ordinary, common-variety apple:

"Apples may not really keep the doctor away," he said, "but they certainly help keep the senses healthy. For the touch the apple offers a shape that invites you to curl your hand around it. For a visual treat, the apple tree offers beautiful blossoms in the spring, the distinctive green of its leaf in summer, the bright contrasts of the fruit-full orchard in fall, the gnarled, bare branches in winter . . . for the palate, tastes from tart to sweet. . . . But best of all, perhaps, is the bite. That first sweet juicy snap of a Stayman makes a moment to be savored."

All that from an apple, the kind that grows in my own backyard? Apparently it's not the sights in the world that are so different from one another; it's those who see.

How can one keep wonder in life? Is there some mental exercise we can do to see it all with film-free eyes? Let me share another story from this fascinating *Reader's Digest* article:

"G. K. Chesterton used to live in Battersea, a section of London. One day as he was packing for a holiday, a friend asked where he was going.

" 'To Battersea,' he replied.

" 'The wit of your remark escapes me,' said the friend.

" 'I am going to Battersea,' said Chesterton, 'via Paris, Heidelberg, Frankfurt. I am going to wander all over the world until once more I find Battersea. I cannot see any Battersea here, because a cloud of sleep and custom has come across my eyes.' "

Well, we can't all go on vacation every time our eyes become dull or life seems humdrum. But we can cultivate that sudden thrill, that leap of spirit that comes when we see the familiar in all its mystery. There's no more excitement in faraway places than there is in our own backyards.

Stand and stare at the sunset, for instance. What glory is there in that daily event? How many unfathomable miles is the sun from us? What miracles hidden from the sight of man keep us in perfect balance with the fiery orb so that life can dwell here.

Foster your capacity for wonder.

Robert Haven Schauffler tells of a shop assistant in Zurich who loved to paint but was full of resentment because of all the ugliness he had to pass on his way to work. One day he decided that his taste for art ought to lead him to beauty where others saw it not.

He decided that every day as he walked that ugly route he would find ten pictures he could paint. His walk became a kind of game for him. He began to see pictures everywhere, thousands of them. A pot of flowers in a window; a ragged boy aping a policeman; sunlight making a halo around the head of a frizzy blonde.

Maybe the reason life loses its charm for us is that we're looking desperately for the wrong things. Maybe, as the painter learned, the wonder is there all the time in our most everyday surroundings.

Ruth Stout, a writer, recalls this moment from childhood: "I remember one afternoon I was gazing out of our dining room window at my two elder brothers in the distance. Their dog had just been run over in the road, and they were burying it under a big oak tree. I really hadn't cared much for the animal, but I knew that they had loved it beyond anything, so the tears were running down my cheeks.

"Just then my grandfather called me; he said he wanted to show me something. There, through another window, I saw three buds opening on my own private rosebush. As I turned to run outside to get a closer look at the flowers, and to smell them, my grandfather put his hand under my chin and said, with his wise, blue eyes full of meaning, 'Thee was looking through the wrong window.' "

How many of us are looking through the wrong window, or not looking at all at the gifts each new day of life brings us? As the Lord said, "For what doth it profit a man if a gift is bestowed upon him, and he receive not the gift? Behold, he rejoices not in that which is given unto him, neither rejoices in him who is the giver of the gift." (D&C 88:33.)

Bring back the awe to life. Foster your capacity to wonder at a world that is full of surprise and mysteries. Have you ever realized the great delight of being able to taste? Have you ever turned off all the noise and really listened? Most of the things we so breathlessly search for are not worth one of the treasures we already have. It is ultimate wisdom to realize that.

If you would stay young, if you would live a life of continual interest and amazement, refuse to be blasé. Refuse to look at the world with dull, lifeless eyes.

Chesterton said, "The world will never starve for want of wonders but only for want of wonder." God bless us to see and know the wonders of life.

In Praise
of Praise

A wife, needing help to get along with a grumpy husband, enrolled in a marriage improvement class. At one session the teacher suggested that all the class members go home and give their partners a sincere compliment, that they should point up something special, unique, or noteworthy about that person they knew best.

"I can't do that," thought the wife. "I can't think of one nice thing to say about him. He's a slob; he's lost his looks; he's fat; he watches too much TV; he's got a lackluster job; he shows me no emotion. What in the world could I praise him for?"

The days passed, and soon it was almost time for the next class session. The wife, getting desperate, decided to sit down and search through all her memories to find something to praise him for. Finally, she found it!

That night when her husband came home with his usual gruff hello, she said, "You know, today I've been thinking about you, and I couldn't help but remember how hard you worked during the depression to keep our little family well fed and secure. I really noticed those long hours you put in. You were just great."

With that, this man—this grumpy, unemotional man—began to cry. "Did you notice that?" he asked.

The deepest urge in the human heart is to be noticed, to feel important. We all hunger for the praise of others. We yearn to be appreciated. A silent voice from each of us shouts, "I'm somebody." "Notice me." "I count for something."

The child who misbehaves in school, the grouchy clerk, the overachiever—they are all trying to say in their own way, "I'm not a nobody—am I? Pay attention to me. Remember I'm here!"

Did you ever have those feelings yourself? It feels so good to bask for a moment in honest praise; to get a little bit of attention; to be reminded how really worthwhile we are.

And it's a funny thing, but praise is a little like vitamin C: We can't store it up. Somehow we need our daily dose of attention.

It's as Dale Carnegie, the famous master of human relations, said: "Three-fourths of the people you will meet tomorrow are hungering and thirsting for sympathy. Give it to them, and they will love you."

Give it to them. Share a little love. All of us are surrounded by imperfect people, full of foibles. Their flaws may eat at us, annoy us, worry us—but oh, what wonders they are, what quiet virtues they have. It takes just a few words to praise another soul, to light up a day, to say in our own way, "You're a somebody."

Ralph Waldo Emerson wrote, "Rings and jewels are not gifts, but apologies for gifts. The only gift is a portion of thyself."

Almost anything in the world can be bought for money, except the warm impulses of the human heart. *They have to be given.* The French have a proverb: "He gives nothing who does not give himself."

David Dunn (no relation) writes, "Some people may give themselves as an expression of unselfishness. To others it may be a matter of conscience. Still others may cultivate giving away as a Christian duty, and surely giving yourself is the heart of the gospel of Christ, who gave himself wholly."

I respect all of these motives, but I took up giving myself away as a hobby because I found that it made my life more exciting and broadened my circle of friends. I became a happier person. While it pleases me that other people are made happier, I do not look upon anything I do for them as being my conscience or Christian duty or as being unselfish. Unselfishness for its own sake does not particularly interest me. It tends to smack of self-righteousness.

Giving yourself away rids the system of the poison of selfishness and produces a healthy glow that warms the spirit.

David Dunn continues: "Each of us receives an equal allotment of time—twenty-four hours every day of the year. Even the busiest among us has from a few minutes to an hour or more a day which he could give to others in the form of some useful service."

In the *Reader's Digest* Hazel I. Dannecker told this story of giving self. "During a long wait in Cincinnati's Union Station, I saw an attractive girl barely in her teens approach a tired young mother with two fretful babies and ask with a friendly smile, 'May I look after your children while you rest for a while?'

"For nearly an hour the girl entertained the children, then helped the mother to her train. I watched her assist three other harassed mothers, efficiently and tenderly. Finally, during an idle interval, I inquired if she were waiting for a train.

" 'No,' she said, 'I live nearby with my aunt and haven't anything to do after school. You see' — and her voice broke — 'there were five of us, and when we traveled mother got so tired. Daddy was in the war. Mother died a few weeks ago. She always said I had a way with children. So I come over here and help tired mothers.' "

In this experience a young girl found her true identity by giving and sharing.

We are all starving for attention. It's a need that is no respecter of persons. The young child, the old man, the rich, the poor, the famous, the obscure—all of us need to have our worth constantly affirmed. And we flourish in sweet, unaccountable, sometimes remarkable ways under the power of praise.

Now this sounds easy enough, doesn't it? But sometimes the kind words we would say get stopped in our throats. Either we're too busy seeking our own praise, or we're so accustomed to the strengths of those near us that we take them for granted.

None of us is ever too busy to pay his own way. It takes only a second to say a heartwarming "Thank you." Probably no American of modern times lived a more hurried or hectic life than Theodore Roosevelt. Yet even on political campaign trips, when in the hustle and bustle he might have been excused from thinking of other people, it was his custom as he left his private train to stop and thank the engineer and fireman for a safe and comfortable trip. It took but a fraction of a minute of his time, but he had two more friends for the rest of his life.

Can you think of any situation in which thanks cannot be given? You can thank even total strangers with a nod of the head, a gesture of the hand, a grateful glance—in jostling street crowds, in swaying subway trains, at the theater, in the quiet of a church service, anywhere at all—if your heart is saying "Thank you."

A gift. A lovely, priceless, powerful gift you have in your power to bestow every day to those near you, to strangers you may never see again. As one writer said, "Let us be kind to one another, for most of us are fighting a hard battle."

Who can count the private burdens another carries? Who can see his cross? A clerk seems hasty; a telephone operator sounds abrupt; a business colleague is defensive. Who can say what ponderous worries are written on their hearts?

Sometimes, it is when another seems to deserve it least that he needs praise the most.

Want to be loved, praised, noticed, admired? We all do. We can't get enough of it. Then *give* love; praise, notice, and admire those you meet, and you'll find it all returning to you a thousandfold.

"Something There Is That Doesn't Love a Wall"

Surely the most agonizing feeling any of us can know is to be lonely, to be somehow cut off from the rest of the human race, to feel that we don't belong with others, that we are worthless, unloved. There can be no wall so hard as that which sometimes seems to separate us from the rest of humanity. And as Robert Frost said in his poem, "Something there is that doesn't love a wall." How much we all need to believe that life includes us, that people care for us, and that we are needed.

But there are many—millions, in fact—who rarely feel that warm feeling of another's love. They are the shut-ins who can't move from their beds or their chairs into the sunlight; they are the handicapped who are reminded of their limitations with each breathing moment.

The hours in each day are long for those cut off from the rest of the world. As one eighty-one-year-old widow said, "Do you think someone might just come to see me who doesn't feel obligated to?" Nobody deserves to be cast out from life.

An eight-year-old boy was passing a pet shop one day when a

window full of puppies caught his childish eye. He wanted one of those dogs, as all little boys do, so he went home to break his bank and get the money. When he came back to the pet shop some hours later, money in hand, the owner said, "So you want a puppy. Which one would you like?"

The small boy pointed to a puppy. "That one," he said.

"You don't want that one," said the owner, picking up the puppy so its deformed leg was exposed. "That dog will never be able to run and jump and play with you."

The boy very matter-of-factly pulled up his little trouser leg and revealed a brace running down both sides of his badly twisted right leg and under the foot, with a leather cap over the knee. "I don't run so well myself," he said, "and he'll need somebody that understands him."

When we're walled off from the world by a handicap or old age or ill health or emotional trauma, we yearn for someone who can give us a little understanding or a little love to ease the loneliness. We want somebody to knock that wall down for us and show us that he cares.

But what if nobody comes—then what do you do? How do you fight the feeling that you're "out of the running" in the human race?

"The greatest discovery of my generation," said William James, "is that human beings can alter their lives by altering their attitudes of mind." We have the power to turn the tide of our lives by filling ourselves with the conviction again and again that somewhere there is a place for us with others, that the world is a rich place to be, that we are persons of great worth. How we think determines who we are.

A woman was trying on a pair of shoes in a store when the clerk said, "Oh, lady, your right foot is bigger than your left one." With that, she left in a huff, buying no shoes at all.

At the next shoe store the clerk said, "Oh, how nice! Your left foot is smaller than your right one." And the lady bought two pairs. It's all in the attitude.

The world can be a pretty dreary place for any of us, but we have the power to make of this life what we will, no matter what our handicap. Whether we mope, wallow in our limitations, or get caught in an endless obsession with our own pain—it all depends on us. No one needs to feel lonely as long as he has arms to reach out to others. No one needs to dwell on his limitations as long as he has the will to move beyond them.

We have to cast out unhappiness from our lives like yesterday's garbage. Nobody else can do that for us. We are the only ones with that power.

Cuban Ballerina Alicia Alonso danced almost sightless for a number of years, seeing only light and shapes. At one period, she spent a year totally immobilized in complete darkness. But more than anything she didn't want to lose her place in the world of ballet. So, when she got the chance to play the role of Giselle, she learned the role by having a fellow dancer sketch the steps with his fingers into her palms. She then rehearsed them by moving her own fingers along the bedclothes. (*Reader's Digest,* November 1975, p. 205.)

Sound remarkable? Yes it does, but perhaps even more remarkable is this story about a man who reached beyond his own limitations and wall of loneliness to help another.

Two elderly men shared a room at a nursing home in a large northeastern city. The one near the window was suffering from a weakened heart, having had a series of attacks. The other man had fallen and broken his hip. Both were confined to bed, unable to get up and walk around to relieve the monotony of their situation.

Every now and then, when both were awake, the man nearest the window would look out and describe what was going on. Since they were on the second floor, the other man, with the broken hip, could see only the sky.

"The park is beautiful," the one would say. Then he would go on to describe the people walking there. One day he began to tell about a lovely young nurse who seemed to walk through the park at the same time each day. "She's lovely," he would say, "—so young, so alive. I wish you could see her."

This went on for several days, when finally the man nearest the window noticed that a young intern seemed to be coming from the opposite direction from the nurse at the same time each day. They did not know each other, and the first few days they only nodded as they passed. But then, the man said, they began to stop briefly for a chat. Before long it had blossomed into a romance, and they began meeting there on a bench, catching ten or fifteen minutes together before going on to their appointed duties.

The man would also describe the beauty of the park—the green grass, the spring flowers, the tall, shady trees. The man by the window painted the picture as best he could for his companion. Then one night, abruptly, he died, the victim of a final heart attack.

A few days after the funeral the other elderly man asked the nurses if he might be moved to the window bed. He missed so much not knowing what was going on in the park below.

That evening, late, his wish was granted and he was moved to the other bed. The hip was slowly mending, so now he could be raised to get a good view of the park and all the lovely things his friend had described. He could hardly wait for the next morning when he would be able to look out and get a good view of all the sights, especially the young nurse and her intern.

At the crack of dawn the next morning he raised himself on one elbow and looked out the window. There was nothing there but a dreary, asphalt-covered parking lot!

"Something there is that doesn't love a wall." Certainly none of us would choose to be walled off by loneliness or limitations, handicaps or ill health, from the rest of the world. Sometimes we just can't help it. But the power lies within us to knock that wall down stone by stone. A tiny root no larger than a hair can begin to crack a wall; a small gesture no more difficult than writing a note to someone less fortunate than we are can be the first hairline crack in our own wall separating us from the rest of humanity.

God grant us the courage to know and understand and reach out.

Look
Within

4

We Have
Been There
All the Time

Some years ago while I was driving with one of my daughters, the little girl asked, "When will we get there?" And then she followed with, "How much longer will it take?"

I couldn't help thinking that those questions are much like many of the observations we adults sometimes make. We think we will be happy when:

we arrive at a certain destination.

our schooling is finished.

we get a better job.

we obtain a certain income.

the baby is born.

our bills are paid.

we recover from our illness.

we acquire a new car.

some disagreeable task is finished.

we retire.

we are free from all responsibility.

My father used to teach us that life is a journey and not a camp, and he observed that too many people are camping. I'd like to challenge all of us, particularly the young adults and young married couples, to see life as a whole and to enjoy the marvelous journey.

A grandmother who had been widowed early in her life was moving out of her lifetime home. Her granddaughter, about to be married herself, was carefully helping her pack the boxes of dishes and the faded towels. "See that sewing machine?" said the grandmother, pointing to a corner of her big country kitchen. "Your grandfather always left his hat there when he came home at night. I used to scold him about it all the time. 'Just put your hat on the hook,' I'd say. 'Why does that hat always have to be on the sewing machine and mess everything up?' Then one day he got pneumonia and died, leaving four little children and me to miss him for a lifetime. How many times through the years have I thought: 'What I'd give to see that hat on the sewing machine, placed there by his own hand.'

Like the grandmother in this story, we too often let trifles cloud our vision. We nag the people we love the best over little inattentions, small faults, mere nothings in the whole scheme of things. Instead of treasuring the all-too-rare moments we share with our dearest ones, we pick at faults, imagined or otherwise. How many of us say to our wives, our husbands, our children, "Why can't you do this?" "Why don't you do that?"

My own daughter left for college recently, and the eighteen years of daily living with her were suddenly over. Where had they gone? What minute, what hour, what day or night had swallowed all those joyous, giggling, growing-up years? The first night she was away I went into her room and looked at her record player and thought of all those times I had mechanically said, *"Turn that record player down."* And I thought, too, how often in the days ahead I'd be longing to have the music still on.

Why do those sudden moments of clarity, when we realize how precious our loved ones are to us, come so rarely? How do we let ourselves get caught up in faultfinding, digging, or scolding at those who are nearest to our hearts? Is it ever worth it? As C. S. Lewis advised, "Take care. It's so easy to break eggs without making omelettes."

Maybe each of us needs to stop amidst our busy, dashing, breathless lives. Yes, even amidst our many meetings and commitments, and really see—see the way his eyes wrinkle when he laughs, see the tilt of her head as the light catches her hair, remember his dash of humor. Maybe when things get in the saddle and ride us, we need to step back for a moment of clarity. We need to remember why we are doing all this—to remember how much we love who we love.

A young mother was running late to a meeting, one that was very important to her. As she dashed from the bedroom, her little three-year-old kept saying, "Mama, mom."

"Can't you see I'm busy?" snapped the mother.

"Mom, I need to tell you something."

"Not now," said the mother with an impatient wave of her hand.

"Mom," began the little girl again.

"Oh, what is it?" said the mother.

"I just wanted to tell you I love you."

Well, life is fleeting at best. We turn around and we're young, turn around and we're old. Minutes rush past us. We can't stop them or even slow them down in their rush. We're eighteen; we're twenty-eight; we're forty-eight; we're gray. Is there ever enough time to nag, scold, dig, or complain at the people we love most? We fool ourselves if we think there is.

There's only time to stop and smell the flowers, to savor moments with loved ones, to cherish the small things with smiles in our hearts.

Julia Ward Howe was once talking to a distinguished senator. She asked him to interest himself in the case of a person who needed help. The senator answered, "Julia, I have become so busy I can no longer concern myself with individuals." She replied, "That's remarkable. Even God hasn't reached that stage yet."

Concern yourself first with individuals, with relationships, with loved ones. What else really matters? Don't imagine yourself busier than the Lord himself, who puts the worth of souls first.

I remember sitting one night on an airplane watching the runway lights coming up to meet me, and I smiled at the joy I felt welling up in anticipation of seeing my family. I had been away only three days, but it was long enough to focus and fan the love and pride and joy I felt inside me. It occurred to me that no other landing in any other place could arouse feelings to compare. The lights below could be the most exotic or luxurious or adventurous spot on earth, could represent any level of fame or fortune, could even be the landing lights for the return of a space-flight hero—with me as the hero. And still, none of these would produce the level of emotion and joy I felt then, just coming home.

Does it have to take flights away from home, your child leaving for college, or the death of a husband who will never again leave his hat in an awkward place, to remind us how sweet are the moments with our loved ones and friends, how brief they are in the run of time? Does it take these things to stop us in our picking at trifling faults and to cause us to realize the beauty of *every, every* minute together?

"When will we get there? How much longer will it take?" are questions asked by impatient children in the car. *"When will I arrive?"*—a question asked by adults as they face the pressures of life. For all of us, let it not take a lifetime before we realize that we have been there all along, that life does not offer us anything sweeter than the love of family and friends and the sharing of time together.

God grant us the wisdom to know that life is a *great journey*.

Elusive Happiness

Ask any twenty people what they want most in life, and at least nineteen will answer that they would like to be happy. That's the bottom line.

In fact, so important was this idea to the founding fathers of this country that they claimed the pursuit of happiness to be an unalienable right.

Some social scientists claim it is the goal of all human behavior.

So it's strange that happiness, being regarded so highly, seems to elude us like some desert mirage. Have you ever been in the desert and seen one of those watery images that look so enticingly wet on a hot, dry, thirsty day? Have you chased it, only to see it vanish before your disappointed eyes?

Happiness is just the same. The noted Prince Bismarck once said that he had not known one happy day in his life. For years he ruled an empire, had wealth and fame and fortune in his very hands, but had not grasped one day of happiness.

Are we in the same danger?

Never before in any society have so many people achieved their dreams—home ownership, widespread travel, college educations, and so on.

Never before has so much money been spent on leisure and recreation. Over 120 billion dollars will be spent this year on everything from Super Bowl tickets to TV tank games to quadraphonic sound—all this in the name of fun.

And maybe that's the problem. As one psychologist said, "The big question for our grandparents was, 'Am I doing right?' The question for our parents was, 'Am I getting ahead?' But for us the burning question in our lives is, 'Am I having fun?' "

We live in a world where happiness is defined as excitement, not contentment; as escapism, not fulfillment. Think of the ads on your TV set. We are told that happiness is the product of sexier toothpastes, shinier floors, and deodorants that makes us giggle uncontrollably. The average person spends over nine years of his life in front of the television, lured into escapist hours watching wonder women, bionic men, and impossible missions.

Manufactured pleasures abound. We get addictions for double-burgers, wear the yellow, moon-faced smile buttons, and avidly consume books that tell us how to be okay, how to be a total woman or a total couple, and how to own our own lives.

Who can even calculate the billions spent on pornography, drugs, gambling, alcohol—all in the pursuit of some kind of happiness?

How did we get so confused? The prophet Lehi said that "men are, that they might have joy." (2 Nephi 2:25.) But joy is not something that can be bought, borrowed, chased, or consumed. In fact, nothing on earth renders happiness less approachable than trying to find it.

I like this story about the search for happiness: "Historian Will Durant described how he looked for happiness in knowledge, and found only disillusionment. He then sought happiness in travel, and found weariness; in wealth, and found discord and worry. He looked for happiness in his writing and was only fatigued. One day he saw a woman waiting in a tiny car with a sleeping child in her arms. A man descended from a train and came over and gently kissed the woman and then the baby, very softly so as not to waken him. The family drove off and left Durant with a stunning realization of the real nature of happiness. He relaxed and discovered that 'every normal function of life holds some delight.' '' (June Callwood, "The One Sure Way to Happiness," *Reader's Digest*, November 1964.)

How do we find the delight? How do we learn to look at a mud puddle and see the stars reflected there? How can we see each morning as one of God's brightest?

As June Callwood wrote in the above-quoted article, "Unhappy people rarely blame themselves for their condition. Their jobs are at fault, or their marriages, or the vileness of parents, or the meanness of fate. The real cause is the incoherency of their lives. Sterile and confused, they have no warmth to give in work, play, or love. They wait in apathy for a visit from the fairy godmother, and in the meantime try to distract their attention from the abyss of barrenness and boredom within them. The furthest notion from their minds is to improve their lot by tackling some self-reconstruction."

"Happiness is not a gift from the gods," said psychoanalyst Erich Fromm. (Ibid.) Instead, I would say it's a gift from yourself. It is that final realization that nobody or nothing outside of *you* can ever make you happy. You, and you alone, have that power.

"An American writer told interviewers that he had been happy every day of his adult life. He had known, of course, days of joblessness and hunger, nausea and illness. But on each of them he had been able to contact the deepest part of himself, which was operating steadily, soundly, and happily." (Ibid.)

Perhaps John Stuart Mill defined the cardinal principle of happiness over a hundred years ago: "Those only are happy . . . who have their minds fixed on some object other than their own happiness; on the happiness of others, on the improvement of mankind, even on some art or pursuit, followed not as a means, but as itself an ideal end. Aiming thus at something else, they find happiness by the way." (Quoted in *U.S. News and World Report*, August 27, 1973, p. 40.)

The Lord said it very simply. If you want happiness, if you

want to find the real you, lose yourself in serving others. (See Matthew 10:39.)

"Men are, that they might have joy" — that's what the ancient prophet said. He didn't say men are that they might have heightened sensations; or men are that they might have ecstatic bliss. For sensations need to climb higher and higher to keep that same appeal; and blissful moments are only pinpoints in time, not hours and hours of quiet contentment.

No, true joy is that inner harmony that comes when you discover there is more to life than yourself. When you get absorbed in a higher purpose than your own gratification, "happiness sneaks in a door you did not know you left open." (John Barrymore.)

Control
Thyself

You probably remember the oft-quoted poem, "The Fence or the Ambulance in the Valley." A small town in a valley provided excellent ambulance service for its young people who continued to climb the high cliffs and then fall off. The point of the story is, Wouldn't it have been much better to prevent the accidents in the first place by putting up a fence at the edge of the cliff?

I submit that we would need fewer ambulances "down in the valley" to pick us up if we would put a fence around our cliffs to prevent us from falling off. And I can't think of a stronger fence of protection than that of self-control. Cicero said it: "Control thyself!" Imagine the difference in our lives if we more completely controlled our words, our thoughts, our actions. It can be done.

Athletes learn the importance of this principle early. I had the opportunity during World War II to bat against the immortal Bob Feller in a servicemen's baseball game. If you ever want a lesson in humility, bat against Feller. Bob Feller had gained a unique distinction as a sixteen-year-old boy. He could take a 9½-inch, 5-ounce baseball and throw it from 60 feet 6 inches at 105 miles an hour.

Now, that may not impress you, but you go to bat and you're very impressed. To those of you who may not understand that velocity, a 9-inch baseball is the size of an aspirin tablet at 105 miles per hour!

But at age sixteen, Bob Feller had a problem. He lacked control. He was a great athlete; he had tremendous capacity; he was born to succeed. But he hadn't disciplined his great talent of speed, so it was questionable whether he would stick in the major leagues.

Bob Feller became a great athlete, however, because he listened to wise counsel. He had great coaches, and one of them took him aside one day and said, "Bob, it really doesn't matter whether you throw 105 miles an hour or 95. If you will take a little speed off your pitch and put the ball where it belongs, you will succeed!"

In baseball, we call that *control,* and you Little Leaguers know how important control is to a pitcher. Bob Feller listened and became the strike-out artist of his era.

I played high school ball with another sixteen-year-old boy who could throw a 9½-inch baseball 105 miles an hour, but he wouldn't listen to counsel. He didn't learn to control the talent that he had, and he has never been heard of since. It's one thing to be born with ability to succeed; it's another thing to harness it and control it.

The words of a great hymn suggest the importance of another kind of control:

"School thy feelings, O my brother;
Train thy warm, impulsive soul;
Do not its emotions smother,
But let wisdom's voice control."

You know, if you build that kind of fence around yourself, you will really come to know what freedom is. A French statesman said: "Freedom is nothing in the world but the opportunity for self-discipline." The remainder of the first verse of the song offers a great thought:

"School thy feelings; there is power
In the cool, collected mind;

Passion shatters reason's tower,
Makes the clearest vision blind."

There is power in self-mastery. Leonardo da Vinci said it very aptly: "The height of a man's success is gauged by his self-mastery. . . ." Would there be any change in our lives if we would heed the words of the song's next verse?

"School thy feelings; condemnation
Never pass on friend or foe,
Though the tide of accusation
Like a flood of truth may flow."

What a satisfaction to be able to act instead of reacting; to speak only after thinking; to merely question instead of accusing! Plato knew what it meant; he said, "The first and best victory is to conquer self."

And finally:

"Wound not wilfully another;
Conquer haste with reason's might;
School thy feelings, sister, brother.
Train them in the path of right."
(Charles W. Penrose, "School Thy Feelings.")

That kind of control takes a very real and personal effort. President David O. McKay gave us inspired wisdom in these words: "The greatest battles of life are fought out daily in the silent chambers of the soul." Self-mastery comes from within.

I am convinced that every one of us, being children of a loving Heavenly Father, can learn to be master of our minds, our bodies, our spirits. It will take time and effort, but we can begin now—with the little things:

Listening to children instead of yelling at them.

Speaking respectfully to parents.

Treating our mates with kindness.

Expelling evil thoughts when they come.

Controlling our passions.

Curbing tempers.

We can all do these things—not overnight, but little by little, day by day, year by year. Do you realize what we could eliminate from our characters with a little self-control? I've been amused by a little food for thought I picked up the other day. It's a message in and of itself and says something really important about self-mastery. It goes like this:

"When the other fellow takes a long time to do something, he's slow. But when I take a long time to do something, I'm thorough.

"When the other fellow goes ahead and does something without being told, he's overstepping his bounds. But when I go ahead and do something without being told, that's initiative.

"When the other fellow states his side of a question strongly, he's bullheaded. But when I state my side of a question strongly, I'm being firm.

"When the other fellow makes a mistake, he sure had it coming to him. But when I make a mistake—Man! That's bad luck.

"When the other fellow overlooks a few rules of etiquette, he's rude. But when I skip a few of the rules, I'm being original."

I challenge you and me to develop control instead of excuses. And let's begin within our own families. They'll notice and appreciate the difference. And just as important, we'll find a greater respect for ourselves and a deeper peace of mind. As Benjamin Franklin said: "Be at War with your Vices, at Peace with your Neighbors, and let every New Year find you a better man."

Confident Humility

The other day I ran across a little poem which I found amusing and deeply insightful. Let me share it with you.

"Sometime when you're feeling important,
Sometime when your ego's in bloom,
Sometime when you take it for granted
You're the best qualified in the room,

"Sometime when you feel that your going
Would leave an unfillable hole,
Just follow this simple instruction
And see how it humbles your soul.

"Take a bucket and fill it with water;
Put your hand in it, up to the wrist;
Pull it out, and the hole that's remaining
Is a measure of how you'll be missed.

"You may splash all you please when you enter;
You can stir up the water galore;
But stop, and you'll find in a minute
That it looks quite the same as before.

"The moral in this quaint example
Is to do the best that you can;
Be proud of yourself, but remember—
There's no indispensable man."
(Author unidentified.)

Isn't that great? John Ruskin said that "the first test of a truly great man is humility." What a pleasure it is to be around someone who doesn't need to continually prove he is "somebody." What a delight to know somebody great who doesn't even know he is.

Have you ever tried to define humility? What is it, anyway? As with so many characteristics of a noble soul, a definition isn't easy. Knowing that, I have a compiled list of characteristics, adjectives, definitions, and pronouncements on humility which, taken together, pretty well define and summarize that elusive word.

1. A quality of character which Confucius said is "the solid foundation of all virtues."

2. A virtue that Jesus taught by his words and by his life almost as much as he taught love.

3. A word that the dictionary defines as "near the ground; not high; not pretentious."

4. A quality which will enable us to have the Lord lead us by the hand. (D&C 112:10.)

5. A quality which is the opposite of being forward and over-bearing.

6. A virtue found in the person who will admit he makes mistakes.

7. A quality found in the person who is willing to learn from others.

8. A quality which is the opposite of thinking one knows all the answers.

9. A quality that is the opposite of self-righteousness or thinking one is better than others.

10. A quality that means the same as knowing one cannot get along without the help and guidance of the Lord.

Again, I emphasize the importance of humility in our lives—but I do so with a friendly warning that you be sure it is humility and not self-depreciation.

I want to introduce a new term to you. I refer to it as *confident humility*. A contradiction in terms? Opposites? No, I don't think so, because humility is an understanding of our relationship to God, and that is a parent-child relationship. What could inspire more confidence than that? Therefore, we can possess the two simultaneously: *humility,* in recognition of the greatness of God in contrast to our own "beginner's status," and *confidence* in recognition of ourselves as his children and—because of that noble heritage—possessors of ultimate and infinite potential.

This spirit of "confident humility" is felt in a little poem written by one of my favorites, Edgar A. Guest.

Believe in Yourself

"Believe in yourself! Believe you were made
To do any task without calling for aid.
Believe, without growing too scornfully proud,
That you, as the greatest and least are endowed.
A mind to do thinking, two hands and two eyes
Are all the equipment God gives to the wise.

"Believe in yourself! You're divinely designed
And perfectly made for the work of mankind.
This truth you must cling to through danger and pain;
The heights man has reached you can also attain.
Believe to the very last hour, for it's true,
That whatever you will you've been gifted to do.

"Believe in yourself and step out unafraid,
By misgivings and doubt be not easily swayed.

You've the right to succeed; the precision of skill
Which betokens the great you can earn if you will!
The wisdom of ages is yours if you'll read,
But you've got to believe in yourself to succeed.''

Let's return now to the last verse of our opening poem:

"The moral in this quaint example
Is to do the best that you can;
Be proud of yourself, but remember—
There's no indispensable man."

I like that! Do the best you can! Be proud of yourself! But remember that not one of us is indispensable! That's the spirit of every great man and woman. That's the spirit every single one of us can and should have if we are to be successful. That's the spirit of "confident humility."

If you really want a study in humility, just watch children—at least when they're on their best behavior. Some time ago while traveling in the South Pacific, I was privileged to listen to a group of small children sing, and oh, how they could sing! Their voices, raised to the heavens, told of the great faith and love they have for the Lord. What a great lesson in humility. It never seems to matter in what culture I find myself, or what the style of dress or the language: the spirit is always the same with children. That same sweet spirit has prompted me to believe more readily those divine words of two thousand years ago: "Suffer little children . . . to come unto me: for of such is the kingdom of heaven." (Matthew 19:14.) If you want an eternal master's degree in humility, study adults. But if you want your eternal Ph.D., study children and then become like them!

Humility affects so many facets of our lives. It permeates our attitudes. It gives life to our spirits. It seems such a small thing, and yet is so important.

Did you ever have an experience like this one that happened to me some years ago? It was late at night and we were taking some of our family home after having been out to dinner. We'd traveled several miles—our trusty car running as smoothly as one could wish—when, as we started up a steep hill, and without any warning, the engine began to knock. The steering wheel shook in my hands and the car began to shake all over as though it had a nervous chill. We managed to get to the top of the hill and deposit our passengers at their homes. We then coasted back down the hill, and with much shaking and sputtering we finally reached our home in safety.

The next morning, with two long trips scheduled for the day, I drove the car into a nearby station and watched as the mechanic lifted the hood and applied the side of a screwdriver to the engine in an effort to locate the trouble. Finally, stopping at one point, he unfastened a wire, removed a spark plug, and, after examining it carefully, looked up and said, "It's cracked."

"You mean the spark plug is cracked?"

"Yes," he said, "and that is the cause of all your difficulty."

"A single crack in a little spark plug could change the behavior of an entire car?"

"Well, if you don't believe it, I'll show you." Taking out a new spark plug, he screwed it in, fastened the wire, put down the hood, and said, "Now go out and see for yourself whether I've told you the truth."

Well, I discovered immediately that he knew his business. And as I drove home enjoying the smooth, even tone of a properly running engine, noting the difference between its present condition and that of the old lumber wagon I had driven into the station a few moments before, I began to think of the effect such a small crack in such a small part had on my entire car—in fact, it affected my progress, my mood, my very life. Such it is with humility.

As we go about our daily labors, let's remember that experience I had with my car. Let's be whole and complete and happy. Jesus said, "Blessed are the meek. . . ." (Matthew 5:5.) And President Spencer W. Kimball has said, "Spirituality comes through humility."

May we be so fortunate as to receive the blessings that come to the humble. And may one of the greatest of those blessings be that of increased spirituality, which brings happiness. May we have in our lives, increasingly, "confident humility."

Humility— Who Needs It?

We live in an age of self-help books. For $1.95 you can find out how to make a fortune, how to be your own best friend, how to intimidate your business associates, or how to color-code your house to match your personality. It's all in the books.

But have you ever seen a book on how to be humble in ten easy lessons? You probably won't. It just wouldn't sell. Somehow humility sounds vaguely desirable but not really compelling. It might help in getting to heaven, but not in getting a raise. In fact, if someone said you were humble, you might take it as a dubious compliment.

Maybe the reason more of us don't seek after humility is that we don't really know what it means. It somehow sounds spineless, spiritless, and incompatible with a vigorous intellect and personality.

Not so. It's a tough, confident characteristic. Take, for instance, Jesus, the character whose life we most commonly associate with humility. He was never spiritless. This one man, with only a cord whip, drove a horde of money changers from the temple. This same man put an angry, emotional mob to flight when they were ready to stone an adulteress. And it was he who stood alone, unbending, as his accusers mocked and condemned him. One can obviously be humble and courageous at the same time.

So what is this thing called humility? It's the realization—not with pain, but with joy—that all virtues and abilities are not lodged in yourself; it's that sudden insight that every soul in this world can be your teacher no matter how low his light burns; it's that intake of breath when you stand before the ocean and realize how vast nature is.

As one writer said, "The job of humility is not to make us feel small, but to expand our capacity for appreciation, awe, delight; to stand silent before all that we do not know—and then to get on with the work of finding out." (Michael Drury, *Christian Herald,* September 1961.)

The Ozark mountain people say it this way: "A man don't know nothin' he hasn't learned." (Ibid.)

Humility, after all, is a question of perspective, an accurate sizing up of where you are in the scheme of things. It is not a characteristic of the servile, the down-and-out, the fawning, the dim-witted; it is that which marks the very finest fiber of man, for it is only the truly great who can begin to size up just how infinite and wondrous the scheme of things really is, how limited any single human is.

None of us is self-sufficient. Shakespeare borrowed plots for his plays; Mozart took part of *The Magic Flute* from a Clementi sonata; every scientist stands on the shoulders of the giants before him.

Yet how easy it is for us to believe *we* are the measure of all things. We begin to think like the children of Israel who said to Moses, "My power and the might of mine hand hath gotten me this wealth." (Deuteronomy 8:17.)

We say, "My brilliance is responsible for this idea"; or, "My own hands pulled us through this time"; or, "My eyes see all that is important in the world—my brain comprehends all necessary things."

Even a college education cannot overcome the weakening

effects of such false pride. Note the case of a business corporation that chose one hundred college graduates, trained them in their work, and sent them out—only to see practically all of them fail. When asked the reason for the graduates' failure, the president of the corporation said, "They thought they knew too much." When asked if his company would stop using college graduates, the president replied, "No, but we shall wait until they have been out of school for at least a year, so they will have a chance to mellow."

We see this same false pride at work in this story told by Bennett Cerf: "The late Bishop Edwin Hughes once delivered a rousing sermon on 'God's Ownership' that put a rich parishioner's nose out of joint. The wealthy man took the bishop out for lunch, and then walked him through his elaborate gardens, woodlands, and farm. 'Now are you going to tell me,' he demanded when the tour was completed, 'that all this land does not belong to me?'

"Bishop Hughes smiled and suggested, 'Ask me that same question a hundred years from now.' " (*Reader's Digest*, March 1961, p. 31.)

In the final analysis, we are all born naked and ignorant. We are dependent on the Lord for every breath, every talent, every capacity. The Prophet Joseph Smith posed these questions: "What art thou, O man, but dust? And from whom receivest thou thy power and blessings, but from God?" (*History of the Church*, 3:384.)

I say this, not to make any of us feel unimportant, but to help us glory that there is a supreme, eternal Creator who takes notice of us. He who at a stroke can turn the tides or create a world; he whose intelligence pierces every secret of science; he whose glory is beyond our deepest imaginings takes notice of us, claims us as his own, his greatest work. He asks us to call on him to expand ourselves and offers to turn our weaknesses into strengths.

Henry David Thoreau wrote, "Humility, like darkness, reveals the heavenly lights."

It is Jesus Christ who, more than any other soul who has walked the earth, we associate with humility. And it is he who had the most reason to comprehend the greatness of God. Surely that should tell us something.

In the midst of his greatest miracles, he went to his Father in mighty prayer. He had been preaching on a hillside, and his thousands of followers began to grow hungry. He fed them with the miracle of the loaves and fishes, a marvelous triumph for him. And in that hour, ". . . he went up into a mountain apart to pray." (Matthew 14:23.) Given the strength he found in talking to God, the next day he walked on the water and calmed the storm on Galilee.

Before one of Christ's most important earthly decisions, the choosing of his twelve apostles, Luke tells us that Jesus "continued all night in prayer to God." (Luke 6:12.)

Michael Drury tells this story about a visit home. "My mother," he said, "lives on a mountain, where in the summer the stars are as big as chrysanthemums and, to my city-trained eye, almost frighteningly close. One night some years ago as we stood under them, simply looking, I was moved by what I supposed was humility to say, 'Doesn't it make you feel insignificant?'

" 'No,' his mother answered, 'only grateful to be included in such a universe.' " (*Christian Herald,* September 1961.)

And that's why we should seek humility, maybe the highest virtue of them all—not to be frustrated by our limitations, but to be filled with a new appreciation and an enhanced sense of awe and love for our universe, our fellowmen, and our God.

Prayer

As my children have grown up, I have had many moving and effective conversations with each one. Those private chats have brought us close together. They have been special times. Problems have been discussed, solutions offered, and comfort given. These two-way conversations have blessed our lives.

It seems to me that prayer is similiar to those experiences. Certainly prayer is one of the most widely discussed of all religious topics. It is discussed by the religious and nonreligious alike. Thousands of pages have been written on the subject; books abound on prayer and its implications. Techniques are suggested in abundance. Much of this information is good and helpful. But I wonder sometimes if the power of prayer is not found in its simplicity; in its sincerity.

Children have a way of defining and understanding prayer. Just consider the following statements from a group of five-year-olds. Their definitions come pretty close to home.

"Prayer is to close your eyes and think."

"Prayer is to bow your head and close your eyes while someone else talks."

"Prayer is when you quietly yell for Heavenly Father to help you."

"Prayer is to tell Heavenly Father thanks for such a nice earth."

"Prayer is to thank him for all of our food and ask him to bless it."

"Prayer is to tell Heavenly Father that you are afraid and wait while he protects you."

"Prayer is to ask him to help you do something that you think you can't do."

"Prayer is the talking we do when we are almost asleep."

Aren't those great? Such faith!

Another excellent definition of prayer comes from one of our hymns. James Montgomery penned these words:

> "Prayer is the soul's sincere desire,
>   Uttered or unexpressed,
> The motion of a hidden fire
>   That trembles in the breast.
>
> "Prayer is the burden of a sigh,
>   The falling of a tear,
> The upward glancing of an eye,
>   When none but God is near.
>
> "Prayer is the simplest form of speech
>   That infant lips can try,
> Prayer, the sublimest strains that reach
>   The Majesty on high.
>
> "Prayer is the Christian's vital breath,
>   The Christian's native air;
> His watchword at the gates of death;
>   He enters heaven with prayer."

I sometimes wonder why we don't pray as often as we should; why some don't pray at all. Certainly a loving Father and his Son Jesus Christ have invited, even commanded, us to do so. To Adam the Lord said, "Thou shalt repent and call upon God in the name of the Son forevermore." (Moses 5:8.) I have heard it said more than once, "Oh, I'm not good enough to pray. God won't listen to me." Ever hear that? It seems to me they suffer from the "Huckleberry Finn syndrome." Remember Huck? Recall with me his experience with prayer:

" . . . I about made up my mind to pray and see if I couldn't try to quit being the kind of boy I was and be better. So I kneeled down. But the words wouldn't come. Why wouldn't they? It warn't no use to try and hide it from Him . . . I knowed very well why they wouldn't come. It was because my heart warn't right; it was because I warn't square; it was because I was playing double. I was letting on to give up sin, but away inside of me I was holding on to the biggest one of all. I was trying to make my mouth say I would do the right thing and the clean thing . . . but deep down in me, I knowed it was a lie, and He knowed it. You can't pray a lie—I found that out."

Either our real or imagined imperfect state stops us cold. If our state is real, then a loving Heavenly Father will give us the desire and strength to change if we ask him. If our poor state is imagined, he will help us see ourselves in our eternal light—if we ask him to do so. The important thing is to try! To reach out! To ask him humbly and simply. I recall a poem which, in a humorous way, helps us to see the importance of sincerely trying.

An Informal Prayer

" 'The proper way for a man to pray,'
    said Deacon Lemuel Keys,
'And the only proper attitude,
    is down upon his knees.'
'No, I should say the way to pray,'
    said Reverend Dr. Wise,
'Is standing straight with outstretched arms
    and rapt and upturned eyes.'

" 'Oh, no, no, no,' said Elder Snow;
    'Such posture is too proud.
'A man should pray with eyes fast closed,
    and head contritely bowed.'

'It seems to me his hands should be
    austerely clasped in front,
With both thumbs pointed toward the ground,'
    said Reverend Dr. Hunt.

" 'Last year I fell in Hodgkin's well,
    head first,' said Cyrus Brown.
'With both my heels a-stickin' up,
    my head a-pointin' down.
And I made a prayer right then and there;
    best prayer I ever said.
The prayin'est prayer I ever prayed,
    a-standin' on my head.' "

Our circumstances, our weaknesses, are not paramount to the Lord. He is willing and able to take us as we are and make us what we can become—what he *knows* we can become. He is literally our Father. He sent us down here, and he wants us back. And in the meantime he wants us to be happy and peaceful. He has promised his Spirit to those who seek it in humble prayer and righteous living. Those two elements go hand in hand. Each strengthens the other.

We haven't discussed here the techniques of prayer, but I can testify that you can establish a personal relationship with your Heavenly Father if you are willing to pay the price. If you desire, you can learn to spend time in his presence each day. Get on your knees and stay there. Learn to listen to him. Meditate, ponder, search. Ask, plead, cry out. Wait, be patient, receive.

Let me share with you the testimony of President Marion G. Romney: "In these uneasy days there is comfort and strength in the knowledge that God is not a distant, indefinable abstraction but a loving, understanding parent so near that we can have daily communication with him."

May we seek after him. May we find that communication which will enable us to endure all things now and obtain eternal life in his presence.

Attitude

Football coach Frank Leahy, a born worrier, never predicted victory before a game. Once when he was coach at Boston College, his team was en route to New Orleans by train to play Tulane. Throughout the trip south, Leahy lamented to sportswriters, "How can we be expected to win this game? We're cooped up on a train, watching our muscles stiffen, while the Tulane boys are getting into top shape with daily scrimmages."

A few weeks later, Boston College was to play host to a team from the West. This time Leahy moaned, "A fat chance we have to win this one! We'll be worn out from constant practice, and they'll be fit and rested after a relaxing train ride."

Do you ever get feeling a little like this football coach—"A fat chance I have to win this one!"? It's easy to moan about the things that come our way. You know what I mean. Your car doesn't start the day you have to be somewhere special, or you get in a traffic jam on your way there. Or it rains the day you plan an outing, or your dinner burns when company's due.

We can easily become believers in Murphy's law—if anything can go wrong, it will.

There's no doubt that life offers each of us some awfully gloomy days. Gloomy for small reasons—the nuisances that tear at our nerves, the traumas of life that tear at our souls.

But no matter what haunts you, what pounds at you from outside with many blows, you have the last word as to how those blows will hurt, or if they will affect you at all.

Contemplate what a marvelous power that is. An unmatchable, awesome power. You cannot control what might happen in your life. But you can control totally the set of your soul. Nothing can hurt you. Nobody, no power, no misfortune can daunt you if you but decide. As one writer said, "The wind that fills my sails propels; but I am helmsman."

I am helmsman of my soul. I will not be controlled by events outside myself. What happens *to* me is less significant than what happens *within* me. All of us need to come to this overwhelming realization, a realization that gives us energy to escape beyond our days to greatness.

Mark Twain said it this way: "Life does not consist mainly— or even largely—of facts and happenings. It consists mainly of the storm of thoughts that is forever blowing through one's head."

Do you remember this verse?

> "Two men looked out
> Through the selfsame bars,
> One saw the mud,
> The other the stars."

Or this one?

> "It's only the view from where you sit
> That makes you feel defeat.
> Life is full of many aisles,
> So why don't you change your seat!"

A young girl had twin aunts who looked so much alike it was

hard to tell them apart—at first. But this identity problem was always quickly solved after just a minute's conversation because of the amazing difference in their attitudes. Here are two letters, one from Aunt Harriet and the other from Aunt Hortense, typifying their correspondence through the years:

"Dear Joyce,

"We are having a terrible snowstorm. It's going to go into a blizzard. No lettuce this spring, and the farmers say this weather is to blame.

"Your Uncle Walter couldn't drive to work today, so he had to walk all that way. He can't stand too much of that cold wind and those icy streets.

"Mrs. Brondage, down the street, slipped just last week and fractured her hip. Not two days before, I told her that would happen.

"I'm not feeling good at all, so I can't get out to prayer meeting. Even when I do go, I don't see too many there. Seems like people aren't interested in spiritual things anymore. I've quit teaching my Sunday School class. Those little children make me too nervous for words.

"Uncle Greg flew to Chicago yesterday. I hope he doesn't crash. You can't trust those airplanes. Just read the newspaper—airplanes crash all the time.

"Well, I've got to close as I want to hear the six o'clock news. My, things are in terrible shape all over the world. I wonder how long all of this can go on. It's awful.

"Love,
"Aunt Harriet"

Now here is Aunt Hortense's cheery note, received in the same mail:

"Dearest Joyce,

"You should see the beautiful snow! It's been coming down for hours, and everything is white and sparkly. We've had a pretty cold winter so far, but you know that makes great apples and cherries later on!

"Cars aren't doing too well on the streets, so your Uncle Walter had to walk to work. I think that's great. He needs the fresh air and exercise.

"Mrs. Brondage, our neighbor, slipped and fell last week. Today I took her some homemade soup. She seemed pleased, and much better.

"I haven't been too well this year, but I'm able to get out to prayer meeting once in a while. There are not too many out, but the Lord said, 'Where two or three are gathered, there am I in the midst,' so the Lord comes on Wednesday, even when we don't. I'm still teaching my Sunday School class after all these years. My, how I love those dear little tykes.

"Your Uncle Greg flew to Chicago yesterday. Isn't that something? Just think, from here to there in a few minutes—what a wonder!

"Must close; I want to catch the news. My, when you hear all that's going on in the world today—wars, murders, and what have you—aren't you glad you know the Lord? And that He is in control and cares for us? I am!

"Love,

"Aunt Hortense"

These letters present a laughable contrast. And one can easily imagine these two aunts seeing the same events pass by them—but how different are their views! Aunt Harriet, growing more dour by the day with her little misfortunes, and Aunt Hortense, with the laughing eyes, finding more to enjoy with each minute of life.

And this is the great secret of it all. Life's struggles are pretty much the same for all of us. But if you would be magnificently happy through it all, remember it is *you* who can choose how to feel in the face of every circumstance. You totally determine your own happiness. Attitude isn't just another something; it's everything.

We can't always solve every problem that comes our way. We may be rich or poor, young or old, healthy or sick. But the great inequities in life aren't really caused by these outward circumstances, like so many of us think. The greatest differences between people are determined by how happy they are—and this is in their own control.

The unquenchable spirit of Aldous Huxley found compensations even for going nearly blind. Being able to read braille, he told his cousin Gervas, meant that one could read in bed with the book beneath the blankets, thus keeping one's hands warm on even the coldest night.

Well, whatever comes to you in life, you choose how you feel about it. Life is not a set of circumstances that randomly happen to us. It's as Ralph Waldo Emerson said: "Life consists of what a man is thinking all day."

Do you want to soar with joy instead of being a passive piece of earthbound clay made unhappy by the whims life throws at you? Then remember—*attitude* determines *altitude*.

Courage

When William R. "Buffalo Bill" Cody applied for a job as a pony express rider, he was received with some reluctance because he was "a mite too young for the business." After he applied some persuasion, however, he was given a route between Red Buttes, Nebraska, and Three Cronings, Wyoming. After a hazardous first journey he arrived at the end of his route only to find that the next rider had been killed the night before. Summoning all his courage, Bill undertook the additional 86-mile ride to Rocky Ridge. The round trip of 322 miles was made with stops only for meals and a change of horses. Alone, young and inexperienced, he completed the longest and best-ridden pony express run ever made.

How's that for courage? And from a boy!

Courage, however, has different forms. Sometimes it is a man facing a very difficult situation, such as a battle line in time of war; sometimes it is an everyday thing—a man doing his job as a policeman or business executive. The work is hard, and it is there every day; there is no glamour, but there is always a challenge. The brave men in these cases are the ones who get the job done—every day.

There are courageous men in all walks of life, just as in each profession there are also the quitters. There aren't too many of them, because they don't last—they give in to the problems they face. Things look too big or too tough or as though they will take too much time. The quitters do not work hard enough. The man who is good is the man who works hard; who sticks with the difficult task, works at it, and finally wins out.

It has been said that bravery is a complicated thing to describe. It cannot be measured or identified by color, nor does it have an odor. It is a quality, not a thing. One of the most widely quoted definitions of courage comes from Ernest Hemingway: "Guts," he said, "is grace under pressure." In other words, courage is doing what you have to do in a tough spot, and doing it calmly.

A true story will help to illustrate: During the battle of Leyte in the Philippine Islands in World War II, an army sergeant led a squad of twelve infantry soldiers through some very dense jungle toward an enemy pillbox. As the Americans came out of the woods and made their way toward the fortress, all was quiet. They did not expect any trouble, but suddenly there was a burst of enemy machine-gun fire from the dugout. It was what American soldiers call an ambu gun, which fired seven hundred rounds (bullets) per minute. I mention this only to show that the American soldiers knew at once that it was enemy fire.

At the instant the sergeant heard the ambu-gun fire, he dove flat on the ground, half in and half out of a muddy pond, but with his eyes constantly on the target. For a moment all of the men in the patrol who observed the action thought their sergeant had been hit. Knowing that he was trapped directly in front of the pillbox, the other soldiers quickly took cover. Then, before they could realize just what had happened, their leader was up on his knees, firing his rifle into the narrow slits of the pillbox. Within a moment he had achieved his objective.

What had happened was this: The sergeant had heard the ambu-gun and dropped immediately on his face, which was instinctive; but at the same time, he reacted as the leader of the patrol and did what he had to do. He was not wounded, and he did not go all the way down on his face to hide, as all the men behind him instinctively did. He knew at once that he could not stay face down on the ground because the enemy would pick off his entire patrol one by one. So he dropped only momentarily, rolled over, got to his knees, swung his rifle into firing position, and fought back. The action was soon over, and the Americans had won. What the sergeant did took courage—"grace under pressure."

Courage does not have to happen only in war. Being brave does not mean you have to be big and noisy. It means doing what you have to do even when you do not want to do it, or when it is hard to do, or when you could let the job slide and watch somebody else do it. Being courageous covers a lot of ground. Shakespeare called it being valiant. There are a lot of other words that could be substituted for valiance: bravery, courage, spirit, backbone, fortitude, heart.

If you read about a soldier climbing out of a foxhole and braving enemy fire to reach a wounded companion and carry him back to safety, it sounds right to call this courage or bravery. But take an ordinary situation in an ordinary life: Have you ever had the experience of standing before a large congregation? How did you feel? Were you scared? Of course you were. Who isn't?

I submit that real courage extends itself into all areas of our lives—physical, mental, social, and spiritual. For some, it takes courage to get up in the morning and face another day. It may take courage to start a difficult task; to face the unknown; to apply for a job; to give a talk; to go to school the first day; to give up a bad habit; to quit yelling at the kids; to avoid the temptation of a pornographic magazine. But courage is available to all people of all ages.

And how about children? The story is told of a little fellow whose sister was desperately ill. She needed a special matching blood transfusion to save her life. Her only available relative was her small brother, so the doctors asked him if he would give his blood so that she might live. With only a slight hesitation, the boy answered, "Sure!"

The transfusion was given, and the little girl was recovering when the brother softly asked her doctor, "Now, sir, when will I die?" It took only a moment for the doctor to realize that the brother had thought that giving some blood to his sister would kill him. Yet he had done it. Such acts of courage are performed quietly each day by those we consider "ordinary."

Now, my question is: How do we develop a consistent, every-day kind of courage? It seems to me that the secret is found in the man who had the ultimate courage—the courage to give his life for every one of us: the Master. When we truly come to know and love him, he gives us necessary faith and courage. His words to the apostles are also given to us: "Be of good cheer; it is I; be not afraid." (Matthew 14:27.)

Those words of solace and encouragement can be realized in our lives if we will seek him and strive diligently to live his word. Has he not said:

"Draw near unto me and I will draw near unto you; seek me diligently and ye shall find me; ask, and ye shall receive; knock, and it shall be opened unto you." (D&C 88:63.)

He can give us the courage which will pull us through, faith-fully, to the end. And, in the process, he will give us a common kind of courage which will help us do amazing things:

Speak kindly to parents.

Treat our children with respect.

Do the daily chores with a smile.

Stick up for a friend.

Try out for the school play.

Continue a courtship after the "I do's."

Work more than the required eight hours.

Smile in the morning.

Say "I love you" to those we do love.

He will give us the courage to "hang in there" when we think we can no longer endure. I recall the words of the Duke of Wel-lington in a discussion of British victories over the French: "British soldiers are not braver than French soldiers, they are only brave five minutes longer." The Savior will give us the "five minutes longer."

I bear testimony that he lives and that he is the source of all enduring courage. May we have that demonstrated daily in our lives. I conclude with the inspired and encouraging words of Moses (Deuteronomy 31:6):

"Be strong and of a good courage, fear not, nor be afraid . . . for the Lord thy God, he it is that doth go with thee; he will not fail thee, nor forsake thee."

On Feeling Inferior

Daily we meet moments that steal our self-esteem. They are inevitable. Pick up any magazine. You see people who look healthier, skinnier, or better dressed than you are. Look around. There's often someone who seems smarter; another more self-assured; still another more talented. In fact, each day we are reminded that we lack certain talents, that we make mistakes, that we don't excel in all things. And amidst all this, it's easy to believe that we don't quite measure up in the grand scheme of things, that we are inferior in some secret way.

Underrating ourselves like this is not only painful, it's down-right dangerous, for we limit the range of the possible. We choke off our talents. And often we are dwelling on small faults of ours that others probably don't even notice.

"My nose is too big." "I'm much too fat." "I'm not very smart." "My clothes aren't right." How many of us let secret thoughts like these tear at our hearts? We are our own worst critics and believe others are equally harsh.

One pretty woman would never go swimming—she never put

on a swimming suit. This was a great mystery to her friends until one day she confessed that she had been walking home from school in second grade when an older boy came up behind her and said, "Have you ever seen such bowed legs?" She never forgot the comment. And though everyone else thought her legs were straight and fine, she never donned a swimming suit.

Another woman gave birth to a child with a cleft palate. Through those preschool years, those sweet mother-child times, she loved him dearly. But a fear grew in her, a fear that ate away at her very fiber. That fear was this—that when he grew old enough to go to school, the children would make fun of him, that they would be cruel to him and taunt him for his small deformity. And more than anything, she didn't want her child hurt.

Then one day the inevitable happened. Her little boy was playing in his front yard, digging in the dirt as boys do. Soon, a little girl came bouncing down the sidewalk, preoccupied with a jump rope. Suddenly the boy's face caught her eye. She dropped the rope slowly to the ground, and she stared. Over the picket fence that separated the two, she continued to stare. The little girl just looked and looked at the boy's face.

The mother, seeing what was about to happen, came rushing to the front porch, her fear in her throat. She got there just in time to hear the little girl's words to her son: "You've got the darkest eyes I've ever seen."

How easy it is for us to magnify our faults, fearing the eyes of others too closely upon us. The truth of the matter is plain enough, according to Eleanor Roosevelt (whom everyone remembers for her insight, not her protruding teeth) "No one can make you feel inferior without your consent." (Quoted in *Reader's Digest,* February 1963, p. 261.) So why feel inferior? Why brood on faults, real or imagined?

Maybe sometimes we need to step back and look at the forces that form our self-images, those powerful mental pictures that determine who we are. Do we judge ourselves too much in terms of physical beauty? Time and age may steal it away. Do we judge ourselves in terms of money or position or glory? Favor and fortune are whimsical.

One college girl who was spending all her money on tuition couldn't afford much in the way of clothes for school. "Whenever I get feeling bad because of the way I dress," she said, "I just go pull out copies of old fashion magazines from the 1940s and laugh. Those who thought they looked so chic then look pretty funny now."

Can you remember this very important formula for living? *Crisis plus time equals humor.*

Yes, if you base your self-esteem, your feeling of self-worth, on anything outside the quality of your heart, your mind, and your soul, you've based it on a shaky footing. So you aren't perfect in form and figure. So you are not the richest or the most famous or the wittiest. So what? As Thomas Fuller said, "What a day may bring, a day may take away."

There is a story that when Sarah Bernhardt in her later years lived in an apartment high over Paris, an old admirer climbed all the stairs and asked her breathlessly, "Why do you live so high up?" "Dear friend," she replied, "it is the only way I can still make the hearts of men beat faster." (*Reader's Digest,* June 1961, p. 217.) Many people were drawn to this famous actress even in her old age, not because of outward show, but because her enjoyment of life did not depend on impressing others, her self-esteem was not rooted in anything outside her soul. Did she feel inferior about the wrinkles of old age that creased her face? She laughed at them.

Who am I, really? That's the question each of us must ask almost daily as we succeed or fail, as we live with big noses or thin hair. The answer to that is a glorious one. We are all children of a Heavenly Father. He created us with great care. He is the artist; we are his masterpieces. Our hearts, our souls, our minds have potential beyond our greatest imagination; we can become anything if we don't choke off our own powers by brooding on small faults or by feeling inferior.

The Lord has given us this counsel: "Remember the worth of souls is great in the sight of God; For, behold, the Lord your Redeemer suffered death in the flesh; wherefore he suffered the pain of all men, that all men might repent and come unto him." (D&C 18:10-11.) There, in a few words, is the whole purpose of life.

As Dr. Leslie D. Weatherhead has said: "If we have in our minds a picture of ourselves as fear-haunted and defeated nobodies, we must get rid of that picture at once and hold up our heads. God sees us as men and women in whom and through whom he can do a great work. He sees us, not as pathetic victims of life, but as masters of the art of living, not wanting sympathy, but imparting help to others and therefore thinking less and less of ourselves." (Quoted in Maxwell Maltz, *Psycho-Cybernetics*, p. 45.)

When experience or time tears at your self-image, as it surely will, look beyond the surface. Don't carry an unworthy mental picture of yourself. Believe that the Lord is engaged in the process of your becoming. Believe that in some special way each person completes the universe.

Finding Your Quiet Center

The *International Herald Tribune* reported that in England the Slumberland Bedding Company, whose slogan is "All we promise is a good night's sleep," decided to stop the night shift at its Gloucester factory after neighbors complained that they were kept awake by the noise.

A good night's sleep is quite a promise in these days of stress, tension, and anxiety. More and more Americans are finding that they need to rely on sleeping pills or tranquilizers or multicolored tablets to help them with their sleeping and their living.

All of us have frustrations eating away at our well-being. Even the tiny ones can gnaw and annoy. A traffic jam, a rude clerk, a broken appliance, an unpaid bill, or just running behind—these things can make us wonder where in the world we can find peace from it all—that old sweet feeling of being whole. Many of us feel like shouting, "I can't take any more!"

In this most hectic of times, how do we find the quiet center in our turning worlds, the still point of our souls?

I've heard that "when disaster strikes on British navy vessels,

'The Still' is instantly blown. It means, 'Prepare to do the wise thing.' When the signal is piped, few men know the wise thing. But in the moments of calm enforced by that signal, they find it. Each man calculates his position and checks his resources. By observing 'The Still,' they rout confusion and frequently avert catastrophe.

"So with our personal emergencies and frustrations. Few of us instantly know the wise thing. 'If only I could know what to do,' we cry, forgetting that the order of procedure is: 'Be Still.' " (Margaret Blair Johnstone, "Sanctuary—The Secret of a Peaceful Heart," *Reader's Digest,* January 1961, p. 131.)

When your life seems to move faster and faster, when you scurry among confusions and annoyances, be still. Retreat. Take refuge from it all to renew yourself just as a carpenter stops his work to sharpen his tools. No use sawing with a dull blade.

Taking a few minutes on a daily basis to pause, ponder, pray, or reflect on a lovely scene is not a cowardly flight from reality; it is a flight *to* reality, a connecting with something eternal, timeless, serene, at the very heart of our beings. And after our few moments of precious sanctuary, we have the strength and the perspective to bear the strains and monotonies of our lives with a new grace.

Marcus Aurelius discovered the same thing centuries ago and said, "Nowhere does a man retire with more quiet, or more freedom from trouble, than into his own soul." (Quoted in Maxwell Maltz, M.D., "How to Stand Up Under Stress," *Reader's Digest,* June 1961, p. 43.)

Arthur Gordon tells the following story:

"Not long ago I came to one of those bleak periods that many of us encounter from time to time, a sudden drastic dip in the graph of living when everything goes stale and flat, energy wanes, enthusiasm dies. The effect on my work was frightening. Every morning I would clench my teeth and mutter: 'Today life will take on some of its old meaning. You've got to break through this thing. You've got to!'

"But the barren days went by, and the paralysis grew worse. The time came when I knew I had to have help.

"The man I turned to was a doctor. Not a psychiatrist, just a doctor. He was older than I, and beneath his surface gruffness lay great wisdom and compassion. 'I don't know what's wrong,' I told him miserably. 'I just seem to have come to a dead end. Can you help me?'

"'I don't know,' he said slowly. He made a tent of his fingers, and gazed at me thoughtfully for a long while. Then, abruptly, he asked, 'Where were you happiest as a child?'

"'As a child?' I echoed. 'Why, at the beach, I suppose. We had a summer cottage there. We all loved it.'

"'Are you capable of following instructions for a single day?'

"'I think so,' I said, ready to try anything.

"'All right. Here's what I want you to do.'

"He told me to drive to the beach alone the following morning, arriving not later than nine o'clock. I could take some lunch, but I was not to read, write, listen to the radio, or talk to anyone. 'In addition,' he said, 'I'll give you a prescription to be taken every three hours.'

"He tore off four prescription blanks, wrote a few words on each, folded them, numbered them and handed them to me. 'Take these at nine, twelve, three and six. . . .'

"The next morning, with little faith, I drove to the beach. It was lonely, all right. A northeaster was blowing; the sea looked gray and angry. I sat in the car, the whole day stretching emptily before me. Then I took out the first of the folded strips of paper. On it was written: LISTEN CAREFULLY.

"I stared at the two words. Why, I thought, the man must be mad. He had ruled out music and newscasts and human conversation. What else was there?

"I raised my head and I did listen. There were no sounds but the steady roar of the sea, the creaking cry of a gull. . . . When I got out of the car, a gust of wind slammed the door with a sudden clap of sound. Am I supposed, I asked myself, to listen carefully to things like that? . . .

"On an impulse I ducked down and, feeling faintly ridiculous, thrust my head into a clump of sea oats. Here I made a discovery: If you listen intently, there is a fractional moment in which everything seems to pause. In that instant of stillness, the racing thoughts halt. For a moment, when you truly listen for something outside yourself, you have to silence the clamorous voices within. The mind rests. . . .

"I realized I was thinking of things bigger than myself—and there was relief in that.

"Even so, the morning passed slowly. The habit of hurling myself at a problem was so strong that I felt lost without it. . . .

"By noon the wind had polished the clouds out of the sky, and the sea had a hard, merry sparkle. I unfolded the second 'prescription.' . . . Three words this time: TRY REACHING BACK.

"Back to what? To the past, obviously. But why, when all my worries concerned the present or the future? . . .

"I found a sheltered place and lay down on the sun-warmed sand. . . . I decided to experiment. . . . I would choose specific incidents and recapture as many details as possible. I would visualize people complete with dress and gestures. I would listen (carefully!) for the exact sound of their voices, the echo of their laughter. . . .

"I sat up slowly. TRY REACHING BACK. Happy people were usually assured, confident people. If, then, you deliberately reached back and touched happiness, might there not be released little flashes of power, tiny sources of strength?

"This second period of the day went more quickly. As the sun began its long slant down the sky, my mind ranged eagerly through the past, reliving some episodes, uncovering others that had been almost forgotten. For example, when I was around thirteen and my brother ten, Father had promised to take us to the circus. But at lunchtime there was a phone call; some urgent business required his attention downtown. We braced ourselves for disappointment. Then we heard him say, 'No, I won't be down. It'll have to wait.'

"When he came back to the table, Mother smiled. 'The circus keeps coming back, you know.'

" 'I know,' said father. 'But childhood doesn't.' . . .

"By three o'clock the tide was out; the sound of the waves was only a rhythmic whisper, like a giant breathing. I stayed in my sandy nest, feeling relaxed and content—and a little complacent. *The doctor's prescriptions,* I thought, *were easy to take.*

"But I was not prepared for the next one. This time the three words were not a gentle suggestion. They sounded more like a command. REEXAMINE YOUR MOTIVES. . . .

"In the past, whenever my work went well, there had always been something spontaneous about it, something uncontrived, something free. Lately it had been calculated, competent—and dead. Why? Because I had been looking past the job itself to the rewards I hoped it would bring. . . .

"My time at the beach had almost run out, and I felt a grudging admiration for the doctor and the 'prescriptions' he had so casually and cunningly devised.

"LISTEN CAREFULLY: To calm the frantic mind, slow it down, shift the focus from inner problems to outer things.

"TRY REACHING BACK: Since the human mind can hold but one idea at a time, you blot out present worries when you touch the happinesses of the past.

"REEXAMINE YOUR MOTIVES: This was the hard core of the so-called treatment—this challenge to reappraise, to bring one's motives into alignment with one's capabilities and conscience. But the mind must be clear and receptive to do this—hence the six hours of quiet that went before.

"The western sky was a blaze of crimson as I took out the last slip of paper. Six words this time. WRITE YOUR WORRIES ON THE SAND.

"I let the paper blow away, reached down and picked up a fragment of shell. Kneeling there under the vault of the sky, I wrote several words, one above the other.

"Then I walked away, and I did not look back. I had written my troubles in the sand. The tide was coming in." (*A Touch of Wonder* by Arthur Gordon. Copyright ©1974 by Fleming H. Revell Company. Originally appeared in *Reader's Digest*, January, 1960.)

It's a frantic, fast-paced world we live in. And we can lose ourselves, our quiet centers, our peace of mind, if we don't take time for retreat into our souls, retreat unto our God. It may not be a day at the beach; it may be just a few moments in our rocking chairs, or at the window, or in prayer. And after all, when the small furies of our world beat against us, it is the Lord who can lead us beside the still waters, can soothe our troubled hearts, can be our sanctuary.

Take time for yourself in every day. But most of all, take time for him. Nowhere can we find more solace than on our knees. Be still and listen to him. Let your frantic mind slow down.

Having trouble with tension? Victor Hugo summed up the ultimate remedy when he said, "Have courage for the great sorrows of life, and patience for the small ones; and when you have laboriously accomplished your daily task, go to sleep in peace. God is awake."

Look to the Light

5

Judge Not

Have you ever been misjudged? It really hurts, doesn't it? It is hard to imagine anything much worse than being misunderstood. But there is one thing that really is worse than being misjudged, and that is to misjudge!

Throughout our lives, there will come times when people who are not able to see into our hearts or understand our motives will misjudge us; and that is all right, for we can learn tolerance and patience. We might cry a little or have a little heartbreak, but we can take it. But the thing we should never be guilty of is misjudging others because we were not willing to understand.

The Lord has told us, "Judge not according to the appearance, but judge righteous judgment." (John 7:24.) But it is so hard to look beyond outward appearance. It is so easy to see *what* someone is doing and sometimes so difficult to take the time to find out *why* he does it.

Jim, a young Indian boy, was in his first day at a large school. He had enrolled late and therefore had to be escorted from one part of the school to the other by the principal. As they moved down the long hall, Jim scarcely spoke, and he never smiled. He often lagged behind the principal, and when asked to hurry, he didn't seem responsive at all. Finally they reached the room where they were going. The principal introduced Jim to the teacher and left. When the principal returned to the office, he was asked by his assistant, "Did you get him all settled in?" "Yes," replied the principal with a sigh of relief. Then he added, "That boy is so slow and backward I don't think he will do well here."

The principal knew *what* Jim had done, but he didn't know *why* until the next day when the teacher brought Jim into the office and announced, "This boy's shoes are too small. He needs new shoes." She had noticed the boy limping. Instead of just seeing *what* he was doing, she asked *why,* and he told her his feet hurt. She had him remove one of his shoes, and there were blisters on the end of each of his toes. He was taken to a doctor, who gave him medical attention. He got shoes that fit, and he turned out to be one of the fastest kids in the school.

Yes, there is a big difference between "what" and "why." I believe the mark of a really religious man is that he is always looking for whys, not only whats.

Do you remember the New Testament story about a small, aggressive man named Zacchaeus? He was despised because of his occupation. The people knew what he did; they knew the way he looked. He was a tax collector for the hated Roman government. People didn't like him because of what he did. But when he heard the Lord was coming to town, he wanted more than anything else to see him. He raced ahead of the crowd, climbed a tree, and waited for Jesus to pass by.

Now I have given you a verbal picture of the man. Do you think you would want him for a friend? What kind of man do you think he was, this man who represented Rome? A little obnoxious, maybe?

Anyway, when Jesus came to the place where Zacchaeus was looking down from his perch, he looked up and said, "Zacchaeus, make haste, and come down; for to day I must abide at thy house." (Luke 19:5.)

Jesus didn't just see this little man as somebody who climbed into a tree and was hated. He saw beyond his undesirable occupation, his small size, and his unpopularity and looked upon Zacchaeus's heart. He saw a different man than others saw—a man with a sincere desire to do better in the future than he had done in the past. Jesus went to the home of Zacchaeus, and there the spark within the heart of Zacchaeus began to glow more brightly because of the love Jesus had shown him. He had a repentant attitude, and he said, "Behold, Lord, the half of my goods I give to the poor; and if I have taken any thing from any man by false accusation, I restore him fourfold." (Luke 19:8.) Now, we don't know why Zacchaeus was collecting taxes. We don't know why he had done some things wrong, but Christ was able to look beyond the outward appearance and look upon this man's heart, and he could see that it was good.

People have a great many problems. Have you noticed? The world is full of problems. People don't really want problems. Sometimes they make wrong choices out of ignorance; sometimes through selfishness. I am not making excuses for them. But there are reasons why people act the way they do, and if we can learn the why, then we can begin to work on those reasons, and then we change lives.

So often in courting, young people look upon outward appearance only. It just seems to be our nature to want to walk around with somebody that is attractive or handsome. That is natural and all right, but there comes a time when we need to look beyond physical appearances and look upon the heart and into the spirit. You have all heard the story of the choosing of David by the prophet Samuel. Saul, the first king of Israel, had at first been a good king, but time and power had changed him. He was no longer worthy to be king.

Samuel, the prophet of that day, had been told by the Lord to go to Bethlehem, to the house of Jesse, and there he should find and anoint a new king to replace Saul. Upon arriving at the home, Samuel asked that each of Jesse's sons be brought before him. As Samuel looked upon the eldest son, he was impressed with the boy's appearance, for he was tall, strong, and handsome. He had the appearance of a king. Samuel thought that surely this was the man the Lord would have him anoint.

However, the Lord made it known to Samuel that although the

boy's appearance was impressive, he was not the chosen king. One by one, six more of Jesse's sons were brought before Samuel, and as the prophet looked upon the handsome appearance of each of them, the Lord made it known that each was not the one.

Then Samuel asked Jesse, "Are here all thy children?" Jesse said, "There remaineth yet the youngest, and, behold, he keepeth the sheep." And Samuel said unto Jesse, "Send and fetch him: for we will not sit down till he come hither."

When David entered, the Lord said unto Samuel, "Arise, anoint him: for this is he." (1 Samuel 16:1-13.)

Why do you suppose the Lord passed over the older brothers and chose the young boy who had not been considered important enough even to be called to the original gathering?

Speaking of Jesse's oldest son, the Lord said unto Samuel, "Look not on his countenance, or on the height of his stature; because I have refused him: for the Lord seeth not as man seeth; for man looketh on the outward appearance, but the Lord looketh on the heart." (1 Samuel 16:7.)

How much different your life and mine would be if we took the time to pray for the ability to look, not upon the outward appearance, but upon the heart. How much more we would be able to love our fellowmen. We would tend not to be disgusted with what they do, but we would constantly strive to discern why they do it. You young people would continue to look at pretty faces in your dating, but you would also learn to look beyond the surface to see what is in the heart and soul.

As the years pass, we do learn to look less upon outward appearance and more into the heart. If you are married to somebody with a good heart, somebody who cares, somebody who wants to serve the Lord and serve his or her fellowmen, then you have found the right one. And that love will continue to grow until the perfect day.

I believe the secret to happy living is to see beyond the surface and to try to understand the "whys." Some say we are not to judge our fellowmen, but the Lord has advised us we should. His advice is to judge righteous judgment. I believe a righteous judgment is that kind of judgment we make when we have the proper spirit and see the inner man or inner woman, and there find that spark that Jesus found in Zacchaeus. So many people long just to be understood. So many young people rebel because they are not understood.

God bless us to see the good and wholesome in all mankind and to judge with righteous hearts.

The Second Mile . . . and the Third

A friend of mine, a retired business executive was once asked the secret of his great success. He replied that it could be summed up in three words: "And then some." "I discovered at an early age," he said, "that most of the differences between average people and top people can be explained in these three words. The top people do what is expected of them—and then some. They are thoughtful and considerate of others—and then some. They meet their obligations and responsibilities fairly and squarely—and then some. They are good friends to their friends—and then some. They can be counted on in an emergency—and then some."

That philosophy seems to me to be not only a secret of success in the business world but also a secret of happiness itself. The Savior of this world put it another way:

"Ye have heard that it hath been said, An eye for an eye, and a tooth for a tooth:

"But I say unto you, That ye resist not evil: but whosoever shall smite thee on thy right cheek, turn to him the other also.

"And if any man will sue thee at the law, and take away thy coat, let him have thy cloke also.

"And whosoever shall compel thee to go a mile, go with him twain.

"Give to him that asketh thee, and from him that would borrow of thee turn not thou away." (Matthew 5:38-42.)

If you want to see some interesting results, try this in your own life. Try going the second mile, and then the third. Do whatever you have to do—"and then some."

Another friend of mine recently challenged his class of teen-agers to try the "and then some" philosophy at home. Each young man and woman was to go home and do something positive for his or her family, and (this was the hard part) do it voluntarily. Well, the results were amazing! You'll enjoy some of these typical comments:

"Dad wanted to know what trouble I was in."

"Mom asked if I was sick or something."

"Dad said, 'OK, son, what do you want?' "

"Mom just stood there with her mouth open."

Now, that's what happens when the second mile is walked only once a year. What a difference it would make if we could learn to do what is asked "and then some" every day of our lives.

Willingness to do more than the required is a continual story in the lives of thousands of our Heavenly Father's children. I am reminded of a letter written by a fine young marine to his parents as he lay in a hospital in Da Nang in 1969. This young man had willingly and enthusiastically given up other plans to voluntarily join the Marine Corps to fight for his country. He had walked the second mile, and the third, and then some.

16 June 1969

"Hi,

"By the time you get this letter I'll be in Guam Hospital, and you'll know why I want to tell you how it happened. My squad was traveling through paddies and some hamlets. We had just come through a tree line when we came under small arms fire. I started to run down a path that all but five in the squad had traveled on. Then it happened. I set off a command-detonated 105 MM round.

"In about twenty minutes I was evacuated to Da Nang. I was immediately operated on, along with four other marines who got hit by shrapnel. When I got here I asked a commander about the exact extent of my wounds. He said I would lose my right leg just above the knee and I might lose my left foot. Well, that's the truth about what I did lose.

"Today I head for Guam, which is very unusual, because men who aren't hit half as bad as I was usually stay here four or five days. The doctor said my operation went so smooth that it was just short of a miracle, and that my instant comeback was greater than that—nobody here can believe it. A colonel took pictures of me and my Purple Heart medal, which he presented. They were taken not much more than twenty hours after I got hit.

"Mom, I don't want you to cry or feel sorry now that I came into the Corps just because of this. I feel fine, and losing my leg doesn't bother me one bit (once in a while I have some pain, but not much). I feel deeply honored to wear the nation's oldest decoration.

"Two more colonels and a first lieutenant came in just now. You know what? I got a Bronze Star with Combat V, and also lance corporal. I feel deeply honored to be able to receive this recognition; this is a big day in my life.

"I know that you are pleased with my actions. I feel I've done my best for my country, and I wouldn't trade places with anybody for anything in the world. I'm leaving here in a few minutes. I'll write when I get to Guam.

                    "Your loving son,
                        "Bill"

For most of us, the price for walking the second mile is not so great.

I love the story of Louis Braille. He really learned how to serve, "and then some." In 1819, a French artillery captain invented a method of sending military messages through a series of punched dots and dashes in a piece of cardboard. This enabled the night sentry to receive messages by feeling the cardboard with his fingertips, eliminating the necessity of striking a light. Someone suggested a possible application for helping the blind to read, and the idea was sent to officials of the Institute for the Young Blind in Paris. They saw no value. But some time later, a fifteen-year-old boy at the school, Louis Braille, recognized the potential of such a system and went to work—"and then some."

While he continued his schooling, Braille worked diligently to revise the complicated writing code. He cut the letter space in half so that the fingers could trace the dots more easily. He introduced punctuation marks, numerals, capital letters, and musical notes, going far beyond anything that the artillery captain had ever dreamed of.

Louis Braille spent a good part of his lifetime in perfecting the "Braille system" of reading and writing for the blind. Through determination and years of tireless work, Louis Braille opened the eyes of the blind to a new world of literature, science, history, and music. (Based on Stevens, *Famous Humanitarians*.)

That kind of greatness was reflected in the life of a former president of the United States, Calvin Coolidge. In 1928, although enjoying considerable popularity throughout the country, Mr. Coolidge announced his decision not to run again for president. Those close to President Coolidge knew he was making a personal sacrifice for what he felt was the best good of the country.

President Coolidge said: "It is difficult for men in high office to avoid the malady of self-delusion. They are always surrounded by worshipers. They are constantly . . . assured of their greatness. They live in an atmosphere of adulation and exaltation which sooner or later impairs their judgment. It is therefore my privilege . . . to retire voluntarily from the greatest experience that can come to mortal man. In that way, I believe I could best serve the people who have honored me and the country which I love."

How's that for a lengthy second mile?

Well, we don't have to be a Louis Braille or a Calvin Coolidge to walk the second mile. President Spencer W. Kimball said, "So often, our acts of service consist of giving mundane help with mundane tasks—but what glorious consequences can flow from small but deliberate deeds." I like those words: *small but deliberate*. Many small but deliberate "second miles" add up. As Wendell

J. Ashton has put it, "Every man is a multitude." Or at least he can be. For when he exerts his good influence among many, he is, in effect, a multitude.

Finally, a word of warning to us all. The Lord has said:

"Verily I say, men should be anxiously engaged in a good cause, and do many things of their own free will, and bring to pass much righteousness;

"For the power is in them, wherein they are agents unto themselves. And inasmuch as men do good they shall in nowise lose their reward.

"But he that doeth not anything until he is commanded, and receiveth a commandment with doubtful heart, and keepeth it with slothfulness, the same is damned." (D&C 58:27-29.)

That's a pretty strong warning, but one that needs to be made. How great are our opportunities to walk the second mile; how great our misfortune when we do not. By learning, deliberately, to perform those small acts of kindness, we will bring immeasurable joy to those around us. And then we will find that our Heavenly Father will pay us in full . . . "and then some."

The Resurrection— to a Skeptic

One sound is more terrible to the human race than any other. It's not the sound of brake failure, as one ad suggests; it's not the squeak of fingernails on a chalkboard; it's not even the slamming of the subway door when you didn't quite make the train. It's that subtle, soft sound as the coffin lid closes and the face of a loved one is hidden from view.

How can so much be gone so quickly? asks the mourner. One minute here, alive, vibrant, laughing; the next minute vanished into some darkness we can hardly comprehend. In the weeks and months that follow the death of a dear one, we sometimes panic, straining not to forget the sound of his voice, the tilt of her chin, the touch of his hand—the simple things we took for granted when our loved one was near.

We can't help wondering whether the dead friend or partner or child or parent is lost to us forever.

Take heart with Rossiter W. Raymond, who said, "Life is eternal and love is immortal; and death is only a horizon, and a horizon is nothing save the limit of our sight."

Limited sight. There lies our real problem with that birth we call death.

At Easter, we think back to the gloomiest night the world has ever known, that dark evening before the Jewish Sabbath when the lifeless body of Jesus Christ was taken from the cross and hurriedly laid in a borrowed tomb.

His disciples were bereft, drained of hope, not understanding what he had told them earlier of his resurrection. Elder Gordon B. Hinckley provides some insight into their feelings: "Dead was the Messiah in whom they believed. Gone was their Master in whom they had placed all of their longing, their faith, their hope. He who had spoken of everlasting life, he who had raised Lazarus from the grave, now had died as surely as all men before him had died. . . .

"We can only speculate on the feelings of those who loved him as they pondered his death during the long hours of the Jewish Sabbath, the Saturday of our calendar."

Had they somehow misunderstood his teachings? Had they hoped for too much? Had they been wrong in believing that the Master could overcome death itself?

"Then dawned the first day of the week. . . . To those who came to the tomb, heavy with sorrow, the attending angel declared, 'Why seek ye the living among the dead?'

" 'He is not here . . . he is risen, as he said.' (Matthew 28:6.)

"Here was the greatest miracle of human history. Earlier he had told them, 'I am the resurrection, and the life.' (John 11:25.) But they had not understood. Now they knew. He had died in misery and pain and loneliness. Now, on the third day, he arose in power and beauty and life, the first fruits of all who slept, the assurance for men of all ages that 'as in Adam all die, even so in Christ shall all be made alive.' " (1 Corinthians 15:22.) (Gordon B. Hinckley, *Ensign,* May 1975, pp. 93-94.)

He had answered with indisputable authority the question of the ages posed by Job, "If a man die, shall he live again?" (Job 14:14.)

It was the resurrected Jesus who asked a mourning Mary Magdalene, "Woman, why weepest thou?" (John 20:15.)

Why, then, do *we* weep when a loved one dies? Is it because the resurrection is so incomprehensible to our finite minds? Like Christ's disciples, have we somehow misunderstood the message that all of us—no matter who we are or what we've been—will be resurrected? Does it sound like a wishful pipe-dream, almost too good to be true, that our loved ones who die are not lost to us forever?

Dr. Russell M. Nelson, a physician and prominent researcher on artificial hearts, has this to say:

"Why should it be any more surprising to think we can be recreated than that we were created in the first place? The same laws prevail.

"Doctors don't know how two cells unite to form an embryo; we do not know how the cells in that embryo divide and differentiate, some to become an eye that sees, some to become a heart that beats. But to us the great miracle of the resurrection is exceeded only by our miraculous creation the first time. For me, it's much easier to believe we can be reassembled with the same elements, the same building blocks, than to believed it happened the first time.

"That second creation will be no problem for the one that could do it the first time."

You say you don't know how a person can be resurrected; how a heart long silent can beat again? Well, I don't know either. But ponder this:

For thirty years the most brilliant minds in the world have been working on the artificial heart—and they are still not able to make one. Oh, they can make something mechanical that will work for a few days, but it always quits. They can't find a man-made material that is capable of unfolding a thousand times a day without fracturing. They can't find a surface smooth enough to prevent blood from coagulating and clotting. They can't find a workable source of energy.

You don't comprehend the resurrection? The most brilliant minds can't begin to understand the laws that prevailed in *making* our bodies. I'm just grateful the resurrection is a reality, that no separation between me and a loved one is eternal.

Not long ago, I met Jeni. Jeni, with the hopeful eyes. She was seventeen, pretty, popular, exuberantly alive—and she had only two weeks to live. Cancer was eating away her body and her future. Her parents tried to do everything to stop the inevitable. They called in top specialists to diagnose the mysterious tumor. They gave her expensive treatments. But nothing worked. Over the days, her condition worsened; her hours became more painful and exhausting.

And finally, Jeni died. Seventeen. These are the times when the mind is racked with questions: "Why her?" "Why now?"

I can only say with Ralph Waldo Emerson, "All I have seen teaches me to trust the Creator for all I have not seen."

One writer put it this way: "In a beautiful blue lagoon on a clear day, a fine sailing ship spreads its brilliant white canvas in a fresh morning breeze and sails out to the open sea. We watch her glide away magnificently through the deep blue and gradually see her grow smaller and smaller as she nears the horizon. Finally, where the sea and sky meet, she slips silently from sight; and someone near me says, 'There, she is gone!'

"Gone where? Gone from sight—that is all. She is still as large in mast and hull and sail, still just as able to bear her load. And we can be sure that, just as we say, 'There, she is gone,' another says, 'There, she comes!' "

Honesty

I cross my heart and hope to die.'' Did you ever make that pledge as a youngster? That's what we used to say as kids to convince one another that we were telling the truth. That age-old pledge reminds me of two different incidents wherein two boys were asked questions which required honest answers. These two stories, both true, are separated by almost six thousand years. One young man chose to answer his question with the truth, other with a lie.

The first story involves a fourteen-year-old boy named Bobby Polacio. This young man was involved one day in a test in rope climbing. The test was to climb from a standing start to a point fifteen feet high. The object was to negotiate the distance in as few seconds as possible. The school record for the event was 2.1 seconds. It had stood for three years, and for three years Bobby had trained and worked toward breaking this record. It had been his consuming passion; it seemed his whole life depended upon owning this record. Let me finish this story in the words of his great coach:

"In his first of three attempts, Bobby climbed the rope in 2.1

seconds, tying the record. On the second try the watch stopped at 2.0 seconds flat, a record! But as he descended the rope and the entire class gathered around to check the watch, I knew I must ask Bobby a question. There was a slight doubt in my mind whether or not the board at the fifteen-foot height had been touched. If he missed, it was so very, very close—not more than a fraction of an inch—and only Bobby knew this answer.

"As he walked toward me, expressionless, I said, 'Bobby, did you touch?' If he had said yes, the record he had dreamed of since he was a skinny seventh-grader and had worked for almost daily would be his, and he knew I would trust his word.

"With the class already cheering for his performance, the slim, brown-skinned boy shook his head negatively. And in this simple gesture, I witnessed a moment of greatness.

"Coaches do not cry. Only babies cry, they say. But as I reached out to pat this boy on the shoulder, there was a small drop of water in each eye. And it was with effort through a tight throat that I told the class: 'This boy has not set a record in the rope climb. No, he has set a much finer record for you and everyone to strive for. He has told the simple truth.'

"I turned to Bobby and said, 'Bobby, I'm proud of you. You've just set a record many athletes never attain. Now, in your last try I want you to jump a few inches higher on the take-off. You're going to break this record.'

"After the other boys had finished their next turns and Bobby came up to the rope for his try, a strange stillness came over the gymnasium. Fifty boys and one coach were breathlessly set to help boost Bobby Polacio to a new record. He climbed the rope in 1.9 seconds! A school record, a city record, and perhaps close to a national record for a junior high school boy.

"When the bell rang and I walked away, now misty-eyed, from this group of boys, I was thinking:'Bobby, little brown skin, with your clear, bright, dark eyes and your straight, trim, lithe body—Bobby, at fourteen you are a better man than I. Thank you for climbing so very, very high today.' " (Victor L. Brown, *Conference Report,* April 1965, pp. 67-68.)

Now for our other young man. His story was told thousands of years ago. His name was Cain. And the question he was asked by the Lord was, "Where is Abel thy brother?" Cain knew where his brother was because he had slain him. Yet he chose to answer in a most devious manner: "Am I my brother's keeper?" (Genesis 4:9.) His answer was as dishonest as any that has ever been given—evasiveness instead of straightforwardness, concealment instead of clarity, a lie instead of truth.

Each young man had a life to live and a question to answer, as do we all. Each one chose a completely different set of rules to live by: one lived by honesty, the other lived by lying.

I was interested in what Mr. Webster has to say about the word *honest*. Some of his terms are instructive: "frank; sincere; according to the truth; upright; just; fair in dealings, character, or reputation; honorable and virtuous." What a pleasure to be around people like that! What a struggle to be around those you're not sure of. I remember an incident that occurred when I was a teenager. One day a friend of mine lied to his father, in my presence, about taking out the family car. When I challenged him about this, he said, "Oh, that's all right. You see, I did it because I did not want to hurt my father's feelings." Thoughtful, yes, but an act that made it impossible for me to ever know whether he was telling me the truth or was lying for the sake of my feelings. Even I, as a teenager, could tell the difference.

Alexander Pope said, "An honest man is the noblest work of God." And the father of our country, George Washington, added this great statement: "I hope that I shall always possess firmness and virtue enough to maintain what I consider the most enviable of all titles, The Character of an Honest Man."

It is perhaps a more difficult task to be honest with ourselves than with anyone else, for being honest with ourselves is an inward thing. We do not have to be honest with ourselves to please someone else or because we know others are observing what we do. And yet, how honest we are with ourselves is only an indication of how honest we will be in our associations with God and with our fellowmen.

There once was a crucial game between two small rival high schools. Both towns had turned out to the ball park. A runner rounded third and headed for home with the tying run. The play at the plate was close, and the umpire shouted, "Safe."

But as the runner picked himself up, dusting himself off, he said, "No, sir, I'm out. I was only a fraction of a second late, but the ball beat me and I was out—fairly."

The crowd was divided in what to think, and for a while there was confusion.

A month later, after graduation time, the young man was called to the office of the president of the local bank. "You have a position here, beginning right now," the bank president said.

"But I wasn't even planning on applying for work here. Who gave my name as a reference?" inquired the boy.

"Nobody," answered the bank president. "I saw that game a month ago. I knew you and your teammates wanted to win. For a moment I was startled at the outcome of that play at home plate. I had agreed with the umpire. But I believe that day I was the only person at the game who made up his mind as to what he wanted. I wanted you and that kind of honesty in my bank!"

One of my favorite stories of how much importance the Lord places on honesty is that of Ananias and his wife Sapphira. The saints in Peter's day had begun a practice of selling their possessions and distributing the proceeds to each man according to his needs. Let's read together this account from the book of Acts:

"But a certain man named Ananias, with Sapphira his wife, sold a possession,

"And kept back part of the price, his wife also being privy to it, and brought a certain part, and laid it at the apostles' feet.

"But Peter said, Ananias, why hath Satan filled thine heart to lie to the Holy Ghost, and to keep back part of the price of the land?

"Whiles it remained, was it not thine own? and after it was sold, was it not in thine own power? why hast thou conceived this thing in thine heart? thou hast not lied unto men, but unto God.

"And Ananias hearing these words fell down, and gave up the ghost: and great fear came on all them that heard these things." (Acts 5:1-5.)

His wife soon experienced the same fate.

I can well imagine that fear *did* seize the hearts of the Church

Look to the Light

members in those days. Can you imagine what the effect would be if some of us started dropping dead when we told lies? I hesitate to describe the scene! Yet the effects of lying do take their toll. And though we do not generally drop dead upon lying, we die a little inside.

Unfortunately, dishonest people also cause problems for those around them. Because of a few dishonest doctors every now and again, conscientious physicians must bear the brunt of such unfair jokes as, "Did you really need an operation, or did your doctor need a car?" Honest lawyers—and there are many in the land—are often discounted because of the false practices of others among their group; and so we peddle more jokes: "Since you won your case, I suppose you'll take your trip to Europe?" "No, my lawyer will take it for me."

Let there be no mistake—our Heavenly Father loves truth. And he has predicted the fate of those who do not. To John he said that the unrepentant liars "shall have their part in the lake which burneth with fire and brimstone: which is the second death." (Revelation 21:8.) That's pretty strong language—but, then, dishonesty is a pretty serious offense.

In conclusion, I repeat a term I just used: *unrepentant*. We all need to repent—some a little, some a lot. But there is no need to pay the price of the dishonest. We can repent and do better, and we can be forgiven of dishonesty.

Those "little white lies" can be stopped.

An honest day's work can be begun.

The "borrowed" article can be returned.

Those unused talents can be shared.

Honest effort can be commenced.

For, after all, isn't honesty a product of *all* our words and thoughts and actions?

I want to reassure you that the Lord loves us all. I want to bear testimony that he lives and that he cares. And above all, I want you to know that the Lord has prepared a special peace of mind for those who are honest. There is joy in the knowledge that you can be trusted by the Lord, by yourself, and by those around you. May we seek that joy and find it. May we come to love truth and use it as our guide.

Do It—Now!

President Spencer W. Kimball has on his desk an interesting sign. It reads simply: Do It. My father used to say the same thing, but added one short word: Do It—Now. That seems to me to be pretty good advice, especially in our day and age. When so many of us find it increasingly difficult to get everything done, there are some things so important that we ought to learn to just *do* them—and do them now.

A very successful young man was asked the secret of his success. His answer was startling in its simplicity: *If not I, who? If not now, when?* Not a bad motto for a twenty-year-old young man.

Every New Year many of us make some worthwhile (if not always practical) resolutions. Did you make some? If so, how are they faring? Let me give you a little test and we'll see. I'll read a list of five possible answers to the question, "How am I doing on my New Year's resolutions?" You select the one that best fits what has actually happened.

1. I made a few practical and important resolutions, and I am doing well with them so far.

2. I made a lot of good resolutions, but half of them have gone "by the board" so far.

3. I made some pretty good resolutions, but I've broken most of them.

4. I made a lot of resolutions and have enjoyed breaking them all.

5. I didn't make any New Year's resolutions because I hate a guilt complex.

I rather think James Francis Cooke was right when he said, "Many good resolutions seem to die a natural death after a few days." And why might that be so? Could it be we haven't made resolutions that *really matter?* Or if we have, do we really keep them?

I ran into a great little story the other day:

Once there were four neighbors who lived side by side. Their names were Fred Somebody, Tom Everybody, Pete Anybody, and Joe Nobody.

They were very odd people, and it was hard to understand them. The way they lived was a shame, and Everybody knew it.

For example, Somebody talked about his neighbors, and Everybody was afraid to do anything because Somebody might find out. But Anybody knew that Everybody was talking about Somebody, so he must have been getting what he deserved.

Really, it wasn't very pleasant to live in the neighborhood. I don't think you would have enjoyed living there.

There was the time when Anybody's house caught on fire. Everybody thought Somebody had called the fire department. Somebody thought Everybody had done it, so it turned out that Nobody finally called the fire department, and Anybody suffered quite a loss.

All four of these bodies belonged to a church. Everybody went fishing on Sunday. Anybody didn't go to Sunday meetings because he just knew that there wasn't Somebody there to be friendly and speak to just Anybody, so Nobody went to church.

Nobody was the only decent one of the four. Nobody was very faithful.

Nobody paid his church offerings. Nobody sang in the choir.

Nobody visited the sick. Nobody helped the poor. In fact, Nobody did everything that was needed in the church!

They needed a teacher in Sunday School. Everybody thought that Anybody would teach it. But Somebody wouldn't do it. So guess who finally did it? That's right . . . Nobody!

And then one day a fifth neighbor came to live among them. He wasn't a member of their church. Everybody thought Somebody should try to be his friend. Anybody could have made at least one call.

Now, who do you suppose finally called on him? Right again . . . Nobody.

Now, it came to pass that at the end of time all four bodies died. And where did they end up? Well . . . Everybody should have pleaded his case, but he thought Somebody would save him. Somebody didn't. Now which of the four bodies went to heaven? Oh, you're ahead of me again . . . Nobody!

Now, doesn't that story have a subtle message? Could it be that it applies to any of us? Whether it's a New Year's resolution or simply doing any daily task, the principles are the same. It amounts to *doing* it—now!

Do you remember the parable of the Good Samaritan? A man traveling from Jerusalem to Jericho was attacked by thieves. He was wounded and left for dead. First a priest passed by without taking any action. Then a Levite saw the wounded man, but also opted for the detour. Finally, a Samaritan came along and took pity on him. Let me read once more about the priest who passed him by:

"And by chance there came down a certain priest that way: and when he saw him, he passed by on the other side." (Luke 10:31.)

Now, without creating any new scripture, let me add something to that verse and see what difference it might make.

"And by chance there came down a certain priest that way: and when he saw him, he passed by on the other side. But, taking a second thought, he said unto himself: If not I, who? And if not now, when? Therefore, he went and did unto the man all that he could to help."

Does that make a difference? Someone along the way will

always take the positive action. Someone will always receive the blessing. So why not *us*? And why not *soon*?

Now for just a moment, let's see if we can come up with some practical and important things we can *do*, perhaps as an experiment.

How about you teenagers? Have you ever thought about writing your parents a note telling them that you love and appreciate them? The other night when my wife and I came home late and made ready to retire, we found on our pillows such a note from our teenage daughter.

What about you parents? What if you, this very night, took time and wrote a complimentary note and left it on the pillow of your son or daughter? Just imagine what could happen in our lives if we were to start *doing now* some really important things:

Taking time for that weekend away with our spouse.

Enrolling in that class we plan to take "someday."

Visiting family members we ought to but haven't.

Making and following a specific plan to finally get out of debt.

Controlling that temper that we're sure "will mellow with age."

Studying the scriptures on a daily basis.

Praying consistently instead of in times of desperation.

Thanking those around us now instead of waiting until the funeral.

Well, the list can go on and on. It's pretty well up to us. But what great opportunities we have!

I want you to know that I have seen great changes in the lives of those who have learned to do important things *now*. And I have seen that great changes make great people. You can make such changes in your own life.

God lives and is our Father. He would have us learn to set our priorities and follow through on them. He loves us and will help. He always has. He always will. May we make up our minds to ask often those questions: "If not I, who? If not now, when?" And may we pray diligently to a Heavenly Father who can help us do so. I know it is sufficiently important to try.

The Educated Heart

Nowadays, the truly well educated sport a string of initials behind their names; there's the Ph.D., the M.A.T., the B.F.A, the J.D., the M.D.—we could go on and on listing degrees for specialized skills. But there's no degree given for the most specialized skill of all—giving with an educated heart.

Just what is this rare, unrecognized talent? Let me give you an example:

Last week I needed a copy of an article from the newspaper, so I called my neighbor. He said he'd check in his garage for it, which was a kind thing to do. A half hour later my doorbell rang, and there he stood with the article in hand. "I didn't have the article you needed," he said, "so I checked with two or three neighbors until I found it." Now isn't that a lovely thing to do in this careless world? My neighbor has an educated heart; he has the talent to do kindness with style.

When we faced a family tragedy recently, we received a card that said, "Let me know if I can do anything to help." That was a gracious sentiment—but the educated heart has the gift to see unspoken needs. Do people shout out their quiet sorrows? Do they order help or cheer or sympathy on dreary mornings? The educated heart sees before it is told.

I like this story about a brilliant man with an even more brilliant heart:

"A committee of prominent Chicago citizens waited in one of the city's railroad stations. They were to welcome one of the greatest men in the world. He arrived and greeted them in three languages. He was a giant of a man, six feet four inches tall, with a walrus mustache. The reception committee stood talking about how honored they were to meet him and how the important people of the city were waiting to entertain him. Reporters took down his every word. Flash cameras were busy taking his picture.

"Suddenly the giant of a man asked to be excused. He walked rapidly through the crowd onto the station platform. Coming to an old woman who was struggling with heavy suitcases, he scooped up her bags with his great hands. Then he told her to follow him. He worked his way through the throng and took the woman to her coach. After wishing her a good journey, he returned to the committee. 'Sorry to have kept you waiting, gentlemen,' he said to the astonished group. 'I was just having my daily fun.'

"The distinguished visitor was Albert Schweitzer, famous philosopher-musician-doctor-missionary. 'First time I ever saw a sermon walking,' said one of the reporters."

No one with an educated heart is content merely with sufficient courtesy. Most of us, for instance, are well bred enough to visit a sick friend in the hospital. Someone said, "You call once or twice? So you never call again? Not unless you have the educated heart. Yet the patient is still perhaps quite ill. One there was who every morning used to bring a scrapbook full of funny items from the day's news." (Gelett Burgess, "Have You an Educated Heart?" *Reader's Digest,* March 1963, p. 180.)

Another who visited a sick and aging grandmother in a nursing home used to take little packages labeled with succeeding days—"open Thursday," "open Friday"—so she'd have something to look forward to between the cheering visits.

Do you treat your paper boy with gracious manners when he

comes to collect? I know a woman who treats her tired little paper boy to hot cookies and milk.

Kindness, and something more. Kindness with insight.

No one with an educated heart would give merely to enlarge himself, for often that makes the receiver feel small. A mother of a high school senior went all over the district trying to get permission for her daughter to finish her senior year at her old high school. The family had moved just blocks from the school's boundary in the middle of the year, but no one would grant the needed permission. Finally, desperate and fearing her daughter would feel miserable and ostracized at the new school, the mother went to the principal of the high school from which they had moved and said, "Is there any way my daughter can finish her senior year here and graduate with her friends?" That principal must have had an educated heart, for his very sensitive answer was, "Why, we couldn't do without her!"

Everything can be done beautifully by the educated heart.

"One cold winter day a ragged little urchin stood on a street corner of a large city, selling newspapers. His feet were bare and he had no coat. As he stood there shivering, a woman walking past noticed the child. She approached him and said, 'Come with me, dear. I want to buy you a coat and some shoes.'

"A smile lighted his cold little face as he took her hand. She led him to a large, warm department store, where she had him completely outfitted from head to toe with sturdy winter clothing.

"The boy was putting on the last of his new clothing as the woman paid the bill and slipped quietly out the door. When he finished dressing, he looked for the lady to tell her thank you. But he was told by the clerk that she had gone.

"He ran from the store, frantically looking up and down the street. He must find the lady to thank her. There she was, walking down the street. He ran quickly to her, took her hand and said, 'Lady, why did you go? I wanted to thank you.'

" 'You're most welcome, dear,' she smiled.

"The little boy then looked up into her face and said solemnly, 'Lady, who are you? Are you God's wife?'

" 'No,' she softly replied. 'I'm just one of his children.'

" 'Oh, I knew it, I knew it,' he smiled with tears in his eyes. 'I just knew you were some relation.' "

That little boy was more right than he knew. We are related to God in a most intimate, eternal way. We really are his children, with his attributes in embryo. With all of creation at his command, with all intelligence encompassed in his grasp, the Lord's main concern is still us, weak and faltering as we sometimes are. When Christ gave us the great commandment to love one another, it was a plea for our own happiness, to fulfill the deepest yearnings of our own eternal natures.

Have you an educated heart? Like electricity, like light, like gravity, it's hard to define, but we know it when we see it. It's giving that goes beyond mere courtesy; it goes beyond convention or the proper thing to do; it goes beyond the easy "Let me know if I can help you." An educated heart has a way of seeing with a special sensitivity. It has a way of knowing without being told.

Much of the good we would do, we don't do because we simply don't think of it. Thinking of it is one of the most important skills we can develop on this earth. God help us to do so.

Learn to Receive

If you really want to make someone squirm, pay him a compliment, or give him a gift, or do him a service. Sound funny? The fact is, it may be more blessed to give than to receive—but it is also far easier. Not very many of us have learned the art of receiving graciously. If you don't believe it, pay someone an honest compliment and note what he says. "Oh, this old dress? I picked it up for $10 at a thrift shop." Or, "My promotion? They were just desperate for help, I guess."

We all think we love genuine compliments or gifts from others, but in truth, once we get them we rarely know what to do with them.

When Charles Edgley and Ronny E. Turner were graduate students in sociology, a classmate of theirs showed great discomfort one day when a professor congratulated him for having done well on his doctoral exams. They both noted his great uneasiness and decided to take a closer look at the phenomenon of praise. Their study yielded an amazing result: they found that 65 percent of all the people praised felt uneasy even when they viewed the compliments as sincere.

Why do so many of us feel tongue-tied and awkward when someone gives us the gift of a compliment? The Edgley-Turner study produced some interesting reasons. For example:

"Once the word compliment meant a tip, a gratuity, something one gives an inferior. Kind words, therefore, may be resented. The very act of giving a compliment implies that the praise is—at least momentarily—sitting in judgment. Thus, a high school principal bridles every time he gets a good report from the teachers' union representative because complimenting him today implies the union has the right to criticize him tomorrow."

But the second reason we feel edgy in receiving compliments is even more interesting :

"Most people feel they must return the compliment, just as one feels obliged to return a dinner invitation or a Christmas card. People simply don't like being beholden to their complimenters and want to even out the relationship as soon as possible." ("How to Handle a Compliment," *Reader's Digest,* October 1975, p. 121.)

Beholden. Isn't that a funny word? How much we hate to be beholden or obligated or indebted to anyone. And more, how difficult it is to see ourselves in need of anyone's gift of praise or time or hospitality. If someone can give us something, if someone can teach us something, we automatically see ourselves as his inferior.

It is this kind of false pride that too often acts like static in our communication with the Lord. Some of us hate to be beholden even to him. We muddle through mortality without calling on the Lord for help because we hate to admit that we need help, that we don't have the strength to meet life's crises, that we don't know everything, that our talents aren't sufficient to breeze us through every day.

There is a lovely old prayer used by fishermen on the coast of France: "O God, thy sea is so great, and my boat is so small."

The prayer goes no further. Some say this is not a prayer at all. Yet we have here the groundwork and the basis for all prayer: man standing consciously in the presence of God, man recognizing his own insufficiency.

Why is it so hard to admit our needs?

Learn to Receive 203

The Lord, after all, is the giver of all good gifts. He has told us, he has pled with us, "Draw near unto me and I will draw near unto you; seek me diligently and ye shall find me; ask, and ye shall receive; knock, and it shall be opened unto you." (D&C 88:63.) He will give us wings to lift us above our cares; he will strengthen us to meet any disappointment if we will just open our arms to receive his gifts, if we will not be too proud to approach him with our burdens.

The greatest among us have learned to call on the Lord and graciously receive his help.

Mason L. Weems, biographer of George Washington, wrote that in the winter of 1777, while Washington was encamped with the American army at Valley Forge, a good Quaker happened to pass through the woods near headquarters. Suddenly he stopped, hearing the sound of a human voice speaking in great earnest. As he approached the spot, he saw the commander in chief of the American armies on his knees in prayer. Motionless, the man continued watching until Washington arose and faced again the perils of his job with the countenance of an angel. (Based on Weems, *The Life of Washington,* pp. 181-82.)

Here is an example from President Abraham Lincoln's life when he had difficulties and needed divine help:

"General Sickles had noticed that before the portentous battle of Gettysburg, upon the result of which, perhaps, the fate of the nation hung, President Lincoln was apparently free from the oppressive care which frequently weighed him down. After it was all past, the general asked Lincoln how that was. He said:

" 'Well, I will tell you how it was. In the pinch of your campaign up there, when everybody seemed panic-stricken and nobody could tell what was going to happen, oppressed by the gravity of our affairs, I went to my room one day and locked the door and got down on my knees before Almighty God and prayed to Him mightily for victory at Gettysburg. I told him that this war was His, and our cause His cause, but we could not stand another Fredericksburg or Chancellorsville. Then and there I made a solemn vow to Almighty God that if He would stand by our boys at Gettysburg, I would stand by Him. . . . And after that, I don't know how it was, and I cannot explain it, soon a sweet comfort crept into my soul. The feeling came that God had taken the whole business into His own hands, and that things would go right at Gettysburg, and that is why I had no fears about you.' '' (John Wesley Hill, *Abraham Lincoln—Man of God,* pp. 339-40.)

General Douglas MacArthur, a mighty soldier who led millions of men in the Pacific in World War II, was not too mighty to pray for God's gifts. He said that God ''has . . . often guided me through the shadow of death and . . . nerved me in my hours of lonely vigil and deadly decisions.'' (Quoted in John H. Vandenberg, ''Great Persons Who Have Believed in Prayer,'' in *Prayer* [Salt Lake City: Deseret Book Company, 1977], p. 119.)

The Lord is waiting to give us the gifts of courage, insight, love, and zest for living if we will but ask him for them. We who think it shows marvelous independence to ''go it alone,'' we who admit no need for the Lord, are just exhibiting that same human frailty that makes us edgy when we receive compliments. We're afraid to be beholden, to admit our own needs, so we cut ourselves off from the very powers of the universe.

''For what doth it profit a man if a gift is bestowed upon him, and he receive not the gift? Behold, he rejoices not in that which is given unto him, neither rejoices in him who is the giver of the gift.'' (D&C 88:33.)

So let us rejoice in the Lord, admitting our insufficiencies and our need for his great gifts.

The Promise

Christmas is a season of great promise, a season of joy. We see it everywhere as the world rests from its cares. Lights glow where streets are usually dark. We bring in green pines. Folks walk with a special lilt. "Joy to the world," we sing. "The Lord will come." "Joy," reads the front of Christmas cards we send to friends we rarely get to see. And, of course, the greatest message of joy we know is the one the angel announced to humble shepherds, "Fear not: for, behold, I bring you good tidings of great joy, which shall be to all people. For unto you is born this day in the city of David a Saviour, which is Christ the Lord." (Luke 2:10-11.)

What is this promise that was Bethlehem, that has the power even two thousand years later to make us joyful in the midst of a long, dark winter?

Every child born into this world is a special miracle. A mother carries it with so much promise in her heart. It is the breath of her being, the pulse of her soul. And at that moment of birth, even though she has never known the babe before, she loves it more than life.

But with the Babe of Bethlehem we sense a special awe—a miracle beyond the coming of any other child into this world. The awe we feel, the power, the miracle, is that Jesus Christ is God's own Son.

"What Child is this who laid to rest
On Mary's lap is sleeping?
Whom angels greet with anthems sweet
While shepherds watch are keeping?
This, this is Christ the King
Whom shepherds guard and angels sing,
Haste, haste to bring Him laud,
The Babe, the Son of Mary.

"Why lies He in such mean estate
Where ox and ass are feeding?
Good Christian fear, for sinners here
The silent word is pleading.
Nail, spear shall pierce Him through.
The cross He bore for me, for you.
Hail, hail, the Lord made flesh,
The Babe, the Son of Mary."
(William Chatterton Dix.)

What child *is* this? What is the promise that was Bethlehem?

The Babe of Bethlehem has a great influence even upon those who are not Christians. I remember an impressive experience I had as a young soldier on the island of Leyte during World War II. I was about nineteen years old at the time, and during the month of December that year the American infantry forces had just taken the Valencia Airport, a strategic air base. Our objective for the next day was a rather high mountain pass to the west. Several thousand enemy forces commanded the high position, which made our task almost impossible. As we dug in at the base of the mountain, it was Christmas Eve.

Like all Americans, we immediately turned our thoughts to loved ones and traditions at home. There were about two thousand American soldiers on the firing line that evening, and our objective for Christmas morning was to take the mountain.

Shortly after dark, a cold rain began to fall. Almost nightly, the enemy would make great counterattacks with suicide squads into our lines. One could almost set his clock by the midnight raids.

Around ten o'clock, with some small arms fire being exchanged, a young American soldier, a boy that I had never seen or met, started to sing, in a beautiful tenor voice, "It came upon a midnight clear." His voice on that cold winter night rang through the valley, and the rifles ceased their fire. He continued his singing and beautifully rendered several Christmas medleys. The whole battle line on both sides listened attentively. Then he concluded with "Silent night, holy night, all is calm, all is bright." And something I shall never forget occurred: over two thousand American soldiers joined him in singing the greatest of all Christmas carols. I have heard some marvelous choirs in my day, but nothing which has matched that experience on a mountainside far from home.

After the singing had concluded, and as the clock approached midnight, a very strange but wonderful thing happened—the enemy did not come. All through the night we waited, and still no enemy. The dawn broke, and still no enemy. All the American forces wished one another a very merry Christmas, and all was quiet during Christmas Day and into the night. Promptly at midnight, December 26, the enemy commenced penetrating our lines, and World War II was in full swing again.

That Christmas Day, many years ago, I witnessed a miracle because a young American soldier had so beautifully rendered favorite Christmas carols. The spirit of that occasion had touched the enemy so much that both sides ceased their firing. Just imagine a war stopped for twenty-four hours because of the spirit of Christmas!

Now, if a Christmas carol sung by a wonderful boy will stop a war for twenty-four hours when no one, diplomat or president, could do it, what would a true knowledge of Jesus Christ do to the

Look to the Light

world? What could the world be like if each of us counted him as our friend, our confidant, our heart, our hope, our Savior?

This world may be a troubled place at times. We see large wars between nations and small wars in our hearts. We see cruelty, disappointment, dark days. But there is a promise, a power, that is stronger than these.

The promise that was Bethlehem is that man is not alone on this whirling globe; that God loves us and knows us and will not abandon us; that he sent his own Son to tell us there is purpose to all this; that there is a voice that can whisper a peace to our souls, and to the world, which passeth all understanding.

Book designed by Bailey-Montague and Associates
Composed by Type Design
in Times Roman with display lines in Times Roman Italic
Printed by Publishers Press
on Northwest Antique
Bound by Mountain States Bindery
in Sturdetan "20075" Black two-tone Morocco